THE UNDERGRADUATE
FIEND

THE UNDERGRADUATE FIEND

THE COMPLETE GUIDE TO BREAKING INTO WALL STREET

BY CHIWAN KIM

NEW DEGREE PRESS

COPYRIGHT © 2020 CHIWAN KIM

THE UNDERGRADUATE FIEND

The Complete Guide to Breaking into Wall Street

ISBN   978-1-64137-373-9 *Paperback*

           978-1-64137-285-5 *Kindle Ebook*

           978-1-64137-286-2 *Digital Ebook*

TABLE OF CONTENTS

———

ACKNOWLEDGEMENTS

———

Writing a book was harder but more rewarding than I could have ever imagined. I had little idea the growth, joy, challenges, and new adventures writing this book would bring me. None of this would have been possible without those who have provided me unconditional support in writing this book.

I would like to take this opportunity to thank John Caccavale for teaching me all about the finance industry when I knew next to nothing about it; Josh Jen and Hal Lin for not only sharing their recruiting experiences but also being supportive throughout our recruitment; and all those who were in the Duke in New York program with whom I shared the amazing experience: Kevin Ma, Man-Lin Hsiao, Nick Hibshman, Felicia Chen, Qiufeng Zhang, Pansy Tseng, and Recya Gupta.

I'm extremely grateful for all the people I've met at J.P. Morgan who went out of their ways when I needed them. This book has benefited from the inspiring discussions I had with Matt Feldman, Mike Nowak, Will Boeckman, Ya Fang, Joe Saad, Shihab Malik, and the whole Cross-Asset Structuring Team.

I would not have been able to finish this book without the support and lessons I've gained from talking with David Wang from Blue Mountain Capital, Jongchul Kim from Hyundai Heavy Industries, Sungbae Lee from Hyundai Heavy Industries, Alex Li from Morgan Stanley, Hyuk-Tae (Ted) Kwon, the founder of Coolidge Corner Investments, and Tim Jung from Duke University. I would also like to thank Clara Yoon for the editorial help I received in bringing this book to its current state. I express additional gratitude to Eric Koester, Brian Bies, Ryan Porter, and all the staff members from New Degree Press involved in the creation of this book for providing the necessary support to become what it is today.

Last but not least, I'm forever indebted to my family, Sungjoon Kim, Sein Lim, Jaewan Kim, Sookja Jang, and Sunwook Jung, for their support in allowing me to pursue my goals and for remaining constant in a period full of change.

INTRODUCTION

"Dear Mr. Feldman," *No that's too formal.*

"Hey, Matt," *Nah, I'm talking to a Managing Director.*

"Hello, Matt," *Okay good. Now what's next?*

My eyes stared into the blank screen as I sat under the incandescent lighting with my fingers frozen near the keyboard. I repeated this process of deleting the few words I had on a blank email over and over until I found myself hopeless about finishing the email. I didn't know where I was going with it. I couldn't stop staring at the blank screen, but I knew I would have to continue typing and at least write something.

Matt worked at J.P. Morgan and I wanted everything to go perfectly. I wasn't going to risk any of my chances with him. Feeling uneasy, I continued to draft the email and pressed send. Later in the week, I received a terse reply asking me to meet him in person in the J.P. Morgan lobby.

There was no way for me to recognize him since I had no clue what he looked like. So, amid a current of people moving in and out of the overwhelming number of elevators in the lobby, I put an awkward smile on just in case someone saw me. I then noticed a man making eye contact with me from far away walking toward me. I breathed out, ignoring my protesting heart and nerves, and slightly raised my hand to shake his only to hear, "What the fuck was that?"

Good job, Chiwan. It took you two seconds to blow your chance.

My mind went blank, buzzing only white noise in response to that comment. I let my lungs fill again and tried to regain my composure and grab at an excuse or justification for my lack of words.

"Do it again," he told me, and I repeated my flimsy handshake.

"Hey, kid. I want more power in that hand. You aren't going to survive here with that lousy handshake. Come on; do it again."

I tried again with more strength. He seemed to like it better, but still wasn't quite satisfied.

"I want you to hold my hand and *shake* it."

This felt like my last chance. I grabbed his hand with all my strength and shook it high up and down. He liked it.

"That's what I'm talking about. Okay have a seat."

In those thirty seconds, I could have been just like the traders in *The Big Short*, who never got past the J.P. Morgan lobby. Instead, I'm here now, watching kids who are sitting exactly where I sat when I first met Matt with the same awkward smile, waiting for someone to come down and talk to them.

Wall Street conveys different meanings to everyone. An aspiring Wall Street student may conceptualize it as the engine of the most economically powerful city symbolizing financial power. A trader who lost his job in 2008 may be reminded of the horrifying memories of Wall Street and define it as the crux of corruption and a melting pot of crooked "banksters." My little brother would probably picture a street full of yellow cabs and skyscrapers with a green street sign that says "Wall Street" in white lettering—nothing more, nothing less.

To twenty-two-year-old me, Wall Street meant everything. It was my dream. It was my idol. I fantasized about what life on Wall Street would be like to the extent that my close friends thought I was crazy. I had professors on campus who subtly implied that I shouldn't get my hopes too high. This skepticism about the odds of actually ending up on Wall Street, however, never got in my way.

Today, I proudly stand in triumph. Dreams really do come true.

I started off my freshman year just like any other clueless freshman in college and decided I would major in economics with no other reason than the fact that I enjoyed my economics class in high school. After my first year in college, I took two gap years to serve in the military.

One night during my service in the army, I grabbed a cover-less book on the shelf and that night changed my life.

I don't know the title of the book to this day. It was the autobiography of a Korean woman who shared her story of leaving her safe and successful career at Microsoft in Seoul to join Goldman Sachs in New York. She described the crazy, fancy, and somewhat tiring lifestyle she decided to live in the center of Manhattan and her stories of Goldman Sachs provided me a new lens to plan my future. I didn't know what finance was or what Goldman Sachs was, but I knew I wanted to live a successful and prestigious life at a young age. There was no reason for me to hold myself back, limiting my future to opportunities in Korea. The book was like a switch; it changed me and the path I would take.

Thus, the journey of preparing myself for Wall Street began: reading books and online materials, meeting people who knew more about finance and ways to get jobs in the finance industry, studying the markets, and more. Professionals had a word for this process of preparing for a job in finance: recruiting. It took about two years for me to absorb and learn everything I needed to about this process to land that job on Wall Street––one year in the army and one year as a sophomore at Duke.

I now work in the Markets division at J.P. Morgan. I face the market every day, making different decisions each time. I trade, face clients to structure exotic derivative products, and do different tasks relevant to day-to-day challenges. Every day is different but exciting.

After successfully completing my Wall Street recruiting season, I noticed a lot can be learned from the process. Over the course of approximately two years, I acquired a number of book-worthy insights from recruiters, junior and senior professionals, retired professionals, successful and unsuccessful recruiting cases, peers, and myself. This book targets those in the same shoes I was in when I had no clue what recruiting had in store for me and those already in the process. I hope it serves as an approachable guide for Wall Street dreamers regardless of age, gender, and nationality.

While I'm aware of skeptics, whom I have no intention of persuading and who have a hard time persuading themselves that recruiting can be modeled, clearly defined steps to Wall Street recruitment exist just as there are "mathematical steps to follow to become a millionaire," detailed in M.J. DeMarco's *The Millionaire Fastlane*. Even if you have no interest in working on Wall Street or want to learn about the market in general, I assure you that the following pages will serve you well. Who knows? This book may change your dream just as that coverless book changed mine.

You may ask how this book differs from any other Wall Street guidebooks that offer information on acing interviews and defining discounted cash flows. This book isn't written to share professional financial knowledge but instead contains tips and procedures one should follow.

These tips include how to:

- Formulate your mindset
- Figure out what you really want to do on Wall Street

- Write an exceptional resume and cover letter
- Network
- Study and prepare for interviews

Having been in their shoes, I always wished I could do something to help the kids who nervously sat in the chairs of the J.P. Morgan lobby. While it would be nice to consult with every one of them, realistically, it would be difficult to do so. After noticing the absence of guides on the recruiting process published in bookstores, I decided to fill up the shelves myself in hopes that the people now sitting in the lobby would have more confidence in themselves. So, this book will paint a more comprehensive picture of the various steps of the recruiting process with nitty-gritty aspects of each step instead of merely focusing on important points to hit for each stage.

How should I title this email? Do I use "sincerely," "best," or "thanks" to end the email? When should I send a follow-up email?

I remember when I first drafted my email to Matt. I ended up googling "how to write your networking letter," only to find opinions of anonymous users on a forum that never really helped to answer these questions. I know it may seem like I was ridiculously overthinking this, but questions do flood in once you're in that position. I'm sure I'm not the only one who had this experience and know most people on Wall Street have had similar experiences. That's why I felt the need to write this book, which entails specific tasks and steps.

While this book won't guarantee your admission to Wall Street, I can confidently say it will substantially improve your chances as long as you stick to the plan I lay out here.

I hope this book is an easy read for you and that it becomes a reference tool whenever you need to get yourself back on track. In *The Millionaire Fastlane*, M.J. DeMarco mentions that smart people learn from their own mistakes and wise people learn from others. I want everyone who reads this book to be wise and to learn from my mistakes so you don't have to make your own.

As a fellow Wall Street dreamer, I truly cheer for your acceptance and success. Perhaps our paths will cross in the future. Use this book as a fun, entertaining stepping-stone toward the doors of Wall Street.

HOW TO USE THIS BOOK

Treat this book as a cheat sheet for you to pick and choose the chapters most relevant and suitable to the questions you have at the moment. I anticipate readers will have varying levels of interest in the finance industry, from those who are now vaguely interested to those who already have interviews booked for their final rounds.

I advise you to navigate your way through this book by choosing the stage that seems to best represent you in the first column of the table below and to utilize the chapters marked with a check in the following columns. Read the chapters, preferably in chronological order, and take action accordingly.

The chapters of the book are ordered to parallel the recruiting process, but each chapter can stand on its own. It's important you take in the information *you* need from the appropriate chapters and start acting on it as soon as possible. If you're short on time, you don't want to read the entire cheat sheet when the answer you need comes from only a section of the covered material. Don't feel pressured to read this book from beginning to end.

This isn't to dissuade you from finishing the book. If you do have time to do so, read other chapters. You'll learn new tips and stories in those chapters as well. Most importantly, make sure you make changes to what you're doing if necessary because, quite frequently, people read about something but never absorb and act on it.

Implementation is hard and needs good and sufficient motivation. Picture yourself sitting and looking around your desk at your dream job, the space you have been dreaming of, every time you feel you're losing this motivation. This book will help you get closer to those doors only if you do more than just read it. Follow these instructions. Don't merely read them.

I wrote each chapter to explain a specific stage with three purposes:

- Explain
- Explain its importance
- Explain how to execute it successfully

	Ch. 1	Ch. 2	Ch. 3	Ch. 4	Ch. 5	Ch. 6	Ch. 7	Ch. 8	Ch. 9	Ch. 10	Ch. 11	Ch. 12	Ch. 13
Stage 1	✓	✓	✓	✓	✓	✓	✓	✓	✓	✓	✓	✓	✓
Stage 2	✓	✓	✓	✓	✓	✓	✓	✓	✓	✓	✓	✓	✓
Stage 3		✓	✓	✓	✓	✓	✓	✓	✓	✓	✓	✓	✓
Stage 4			✓	✓	✓	✓	✓	✓	✓	✓	✓	✓	✓
Stage 5				✓	✓	✓	✓	✓	✓	✓	✓	✓	✓
Stage 6					✓	✓	✓	✓	✓	✓	✓	✓	✓
Stage 7										✓	✓	✓	✓
Stage 8											✓	✓	✓

Stage 1: I'm a newbie in finance and am not sure if I want to work in the industry.

Stage 2: I know I want to work in finance, but I have no idea where to start.

Stage 3: I know I want to work on Wall Street and I understand the high-level process of finance recruiting, but I don't know what role within finance is suitable for me.

Stage 4: I know what job I want but I need help writing a good resume.

Stage 5: I know what job I want but I need help writing a good cover letter.

Stage 6: I don't know what networking is, but I want to become an effective networker.

Stage 7: I passed the first round of resume screening and/or am confident with my resume, cover letter, and networking skills, but I need to brush up on my interviews.

Stage 8: I have an interview coming up and/or anticipating interviews in the future.

CHAPTER 1

THE FINANCE MINDSET

"So, what makes you want to do finance?"

This was a simple question he should have known the answer to. To some extent, he wanted to say he was in it for the money and it seemed his mentor read through him.

"If it's for the money, you might as well go to any tech firm out there because they pay great."

Josh Jen, who is now at Goldman Sachs as a trader working with interest rate derivative products, recounted the moment he first met his mentor at Goldman Sachs.

"I felt like he was looking right through me. I felt bad that I wasn't able to give him a good reason why I wanted to pursue a career in finance. Sure, it pays well, and it'd be nice to have a reputation to be working on Wall Street, but is that really a good enough reason?"

Josh's mentor was right. Many other jobs offer similar salaries and reputations.

The next couple of meetings with his mentor didn't work out as Josh hoped. He expected specific insider tips to recruit successfully, but instead his mentor spent hours talking about why other potential jobs could be a better choice for his career.

Josh later realized he wanted more than money and fame. He admired the lifestyle of a trader and the traits a successful trader has. High quantitative skills, fast yet smart decision making, and the concept of managing risk were the qualities that made the job and finance so special to Josh. Only after he shared these thoughts with his mentor did his mentor start to talk about strategies to land a job on Wall Street.

"You aren't going to succeed in recruiting for finance unless you figure out the answer to why you want to do finance. Everything else is easy, understanding the true reason why you want to do it is much more important than being able to write a perfect resume. You won't be able to survive in this world without knowing why you're in it in the first place."

At the time, his mentor's comment seemed to make sense but wasn't completely absorbable. In retrospect, Josh now realizes why his mentor pushed him so hard to find a good reason for wanting a job on Wall Street. His mentor had a point, but Josh knew his craving for a career in finance was strong. However, he wasn't able to articulate it effectively.

One of the most dangerous ways to get yourself involved in this process is to come in without knowing what you're up against. Many people join the industry without a clear understanding of what the job truly entails. I find it quite ironic that they don't really understand what investment banks, hedge funds, and asset managers do, considering how often these topics are talked about. People who fail to do their preliminary research tend to leave within a few years, regretting the energy and time wasted.

This chapter should provide you with guidelines to figure out the finance mindset you need before getting started.

WHY DO YOU WANT TO WORK IN FINANCE?

Right now, ask yourself why you want to join the finance industry. Answering this question *has* to be step zero.

For those who already know their reasons, use this moment as an opportunity to remind yourself. As you get further into the process, it's easy to forget the reasons you wanted to pursue this career. It's important to define your reasons and goals now and it's okay to find your reason based on the vague, ambiguous idea you currently have about the industry. When answering this question, follow one important rule: be honest with yourself. It's relatively easy to bullshit other people, but you'll trap yourself in your own web once you start deceiving yourself.

The most frequent answer I hear for joining the industry is money. Money is important, but almost every professional I've met so far has warned me that if money is the only reason for pursuing a career in finance, it's not worth it. As much as they pay, careers in finance are so stressful that burnouts are inevitable if money is the only motivating factor.

Would you not be better off in software engineering, law, or consulting?

These questions may be posed in an interview and it's extremely important to know why you're choosing the finance industry. I personally found it helpful to listen to other people explain why they started their careers in finance when finding ways to accurately process and articulate my reasons.

HOW SOME YOUNG PROFESSIONALS DECIDED TO PURSUE FINANCE

Josh bought his first ounce of gold when he was twelve. He knew absolutely nothing about investment, but he had the courage, time, and money to invest in gold. Gold was an attractive asset for a twelve-year-old and the easiest one to physically picture. When he heard from his parents that the value of his gold increased after a month, he had an epiphany: free money is out there.

Using the same logic, Josh bought three shares of Apple's stock in 2012. He has kept these shares and his ounce of gold to this day. Ever since he made these investments, Josh has been interested in the market. *How does the value of an asset fluctuate over time?* This question allowed Josh to find his passion in trading, which he has successfully turned into a reality.

Michael Tan, an investment banking analyst at Goldman Sachs, grew up with an interest in startups. This interest in early-stage businesses led him to pursue an internship at a venture capital firm that invests in startups. He later learned of initial public offerings (IPOs) and large-scale deals, which prompted him to learn more about how the biggest players in the field and the overall market work.

I'm sure not everyone can pinpoint an early childhood experience like Josh or Michael. It's fine if you can't. I couldn't either.

In retrospect, I didn't have a good reason for seeking a career in finance other than the fact that many of my friends were doing it and I wanted to live the successful and prestigious life the lady in the coverless book wrote about. But the more I learned about finance, the more excited I became. Every time I learned about a new concept or model in class, I found myself wondering how they were applicable in real life on Wall Street. I soon noticed that this was my passion. The first visit to the trading floor was all it took to confirm that I wanted to work in the markets.

WHERE TO WORK?

"The flag of New York City should be someone with four bags opening a door with their shoulder" wrote Alex Baze.

New York is hated as much as it's loved. The city has become the mecca of finance and is often referred to as a symbol of money and capitalism. The streets and subways are dirty and everything is overpriced, but the buildings are filled with smart and bright people. It's a melting pot of business, art, and food from all around the world and this is only part of what makes New York so amazing. The city is full of opportunities and hope.

Professionals frequently move around different firms and the proximity of these career opportunities not only allows this, but celebrates it. You'll be exposed to different opportunities and all you have to do is make use of them. The scales of financial transactions and businesses are global and unchallenged. The city alone, according to *Market Insider*, produces 8 percent of the nation's GDP.

Despite these attractions, you may still be unconvinced about starting your career in New York. You don't have to choose New York as long as you're looking into a city that shares the same traits. It can be London, Hong Kong, Tokyo, or any other city as long as it's a place full of opportunities. Obviously, preferences for cities depend on each person, I personally value the experience New York offers.

Recruiting timelines differ across regions. Recruitment in New York usually starts in the summer or fall of the year before you actually step into office while offices in other cities recruit in the fall or winter.

So why not apply and decide afterward? Because while it's relatively easy to switch to offices in Europe or Asia, that's not necessarily the case the other way around due to the high demand for positions in New York offices.

Take the time to think about where, geographically, you want to work in finance. Your preferred location may alter the ways you prepare for recruiting. New York, for example, involves heavy networking, whereas in Hong Kong, networking is relatively less important. I have personally only recruited for New York, so I cannot speak extensively about recruiting in other cities, but I'm sure the processes significantly overlap. Even if you aren't interested in working in New York, this book will come in handy.

CHOOSING YOUR STARTING JOB

In the classic game of Pokémon, players are given the option of playing one of the three different starter Pokémon: Bulbasaur, Charmander, and Squirtle.

When I started playing, I didn't know what to choose. *Squirtle or Charmander? Squirtle or Charmander?* I would repeat this question over and over again in my head because once you choose one, you never get a chance to own the other two.

Just like these starter Pokémon, you need to decide on your first job. I know it's not fair to be asked to decide what you want to do without the chance to experience it, but you have resources. Mentors, classes, professors, friends, advisers, internships, and online resources are available so you can effectively navigate this hard but necessary decision. It may seem like these aren't much, but, unfortunately, it's your responsibility to actively utilize these resources to make the smartest choice possible. You can ask for advice and descriptions of what each job in finance entails from those who have a better understanding of them than you do. You can go online and try to figure out the different roles in finance. Don't limit yourself to your first connections; figure out who else you can connect with to learn more about the industry.

Once you decide to start a career in finance as an investment banking analyst, it might be difficult to start anew as a software engineer or a lawyer as these professions require years of prior preparation to become qualified to practice them. But even within finance, it's important what you want to do. For example, even jobs that seem relevant to trading like hedge funds hire more investment bankers than traders according to a senior hedge fund manager at Three Point Capital.

You aren't restricted to your first job, but it certainly will have some impact on your future career options. Of course, some people say it's not hard to work across different industries. While it's highly encouraged to switch industries and professions in our modern society, it's easier said than done.

THE BIG FRAMEWORK AND ITS TIMELINE

I want to draw a big picture that can summarize finance recruiting in seven big stages:

- Research
- Resume Generation
- Cover Letter Generation
- Networking
- Interview Preparation
- Interviews
- After the Offer

Networking should be an effort that's continued throughout the entire time frame. I denote networking as stage four because it's most critical during that phase. *This* is the most generic way of introducing this intense process. This isn't to say that this breakdown of the process is the only way to successfully recruit. However, I'm confidently presenting this method because it's a framework that's safe, convenient, and, most importantly, generally applicable. Other chapters with sections for each stage will fill in the details. For now, note that these seven stages are crucial steppingstones to your finance internship.

Here's a general timeline for these stages. The ideal amount of recruiting preparation is at least one year. This doesn't include the time needed to develop the finance mindset discussed in this chapter. The timeline only captures the time from the research phase discussed in chapter two to the end of the interviews discussed in chapter eight. I understand that everyone reading this book will be at a different stage in the timeline. If you have less than a year left until your interviews, tailor these instructions according to your needs.

In this book, however, I'll walk through the recruiting process, assuming you have approximately a year left until final interviews.

MONTHS 1 AND 2

The first month of your timeline should be devoted to research. In this phase, you're reading this book and going online to conduct research on the field and different careers. This is the early phase when you find out about the different roles within finance and the job opportunities. You don't want to take more than two months for this process. I'm not saying you should stop your research after the first two months, but it's ideal that you have most of your research finished because you have a lot of work to do after.

MONTHS 3 AND 4

The second and third stages are getting your resume and cover letter ready. You should start working on your resume and cover letter by the start of your third month and try to finish this before the end of your fourth month. Obviously, your resume and cover letter might change throughout the process, so don't limit yourself to these months. Ideally, however, you should be ready and comfortable with a finalized resume and cover letter.

MONTHS 5 THROUGH 9

The fourth stage is networking. As I said earlier, the networking stage should be a continued effort throughout all stages and even beyond the scope of this book. Some of you may have heard of networking, but, unfortunately, few can explicitly explain what it is and how to do it effectively. You'll be networking throughout the year, but you should concentrate your networking effort from the fifth to the ninth month. Four months may sound like a lot but, remember, networking never ends. The more, the better.

MONTHS 10 THROUGH 12

The fifth and the sixth stages are preparing for and going to interviews. Firms typically have online interviews and in-person interviews. You'll be working on interviews for probably the last three months of this time frame. Three months will be enough time for you to be confident enough to answer any behavioral or technical questions.

Try to have this big framework in your head and tailor it to the months you have left until recruiting. If you have a total of six months, for example, you might want to devote a month to research, a month to your resume and cover letter, two and a half months to networking, and a month and a half for interview preparation. The stages don't have to be proportionately scaled.

I know it's ridiculously early for firms on Wall Street to be recruiting for junior internships as early as fifteen months prior to the actual starting date. Growing competition for talent has inevitably made firms more actively compete for good candidates and all we can do is play by their rules whether we like them or not. The timeline for recruiting changes every year, so it's important that you know when your specific class will be recruiting.

The breakdown of the process may seem tedious and stressful. It's a huge time commitment. I know a number of people who decided to quit recruiting for finance because of the heavy commitment required during the process. So, again, please use this book as a guide whenever you feel lost or confused.

You might wonder about the degree of commitment required throughout each stage. To provide more clarity, I created a table with a rough approximation of hours you should spend during each stage. The indicated hours are ideal targets. They include anything that may be relevant to recruiting, whether it be the hours spent reading the news, taking finance classes, or simply browsing random finance facts online.

Months 1 and 2	Months 3 and 4	Months 5 through 9	Months 10 through 12
Research	Resume/Cover Letter	Networking	Interview Preparation
30 hours	30 hours	150 hours	100 hours
30 minutes per day	30 minutes per day	1 hour per day	1 hour per day

FIEND VS. FOE

Finance recruiting is tough. A rule of thumb: embrace your inner fiend. Don't feel embarrassed or self-conscious about trying hard and putting in the needed effort. I know at times it may seem important that you don't look like a try-hard. It's better to be a try-hard and achieve your goals than to fail.

My friend and I call the act of investing extra time and effort into finance recruiting "fiending." We call each other fiends whenever we spot each other doing something productive for recruiting. I thank Kevin Ma, my banker friend at Houlihan Lokey, for first using this term. It perfectly conveys the nuance behind the mentality of a person who desperately dreams of a job on Wall Street.

Merriam Webster defines a fiend as a devil. However, it has a second definition as a person extremely devoted to a pursuit or study. We want to fall under the second definition. As the word fiend entails the definition of a devil, being called a finance fiend isn't really the most pleasant feeling. Regardless, the word accurately describes an ideal candidate for recruitment.

The reality is that firms have plenty of candidates to pick from and most candidates are sufficiently qualified. The real game changer in this race is how much of a fanatic and a fiend you are in conveying your passion and interest in the job.

I'll be using the word fiend throughout the book, as it was our way of joking around when I was recruiting. Fiending is good. The more you become a fiend, the more likely you'll land that dream job. So, this book will teach you to become a fiend without becoming a foe. The line that separates one from the other is ambiguous but very thin. No partial credit is given in recruiting. You're either in or out. A foe is an enemy, someone who is out and who you don't want to be.

The goal is to avoid becoming a foe but to approach it as closely as possible. The actions and mentality required are almost identical. For example, if you repeat the actions of a fiend too excessively or aggressively, you become a foe.

Then where do you draw the line?

Becoming a fiend isn't easy. It forces you to get out of your comfort zone and take initiative you aren't used to. More often than not, you'll be rejected or ignored by people you might have thought you had solid relationships with. The emotional and technical steps that accompany the road to becoming a finance fiend require great endurance. But once you win the title, the reward is promising. In the following chapters, I'll walk you through the steps to become a fiend.

KEYS TO BECOMING A FIEND

- Develop a finance mindset: ask yourself why *you* want to work in finance.
- Decide where you want to work.
- Your first career matters; actively utilize the resources available to you.
- Embrace your inner fiend; don't feel embarrassed or self-conscious about being a try-hard.
- Be a fiend, not a foe; find the fine line that distinguishes the two.

CHAPTER 2

THE RESEARCH PHASE

Everyone on campus talked about investment banking and they did a great job selling it as if it were the ideal job.

So, when I first decided to join the finance industry, I pictured myself in a suit as an investment banker meeting different clients. Little did I know that I would end up in a job that doesn't require wearing a suit or meeting clients. I work in the markets division at J.P. Morgan, which is equivalent to sales and trading at other firms. As an analyst who works in the markets, the work I do has nothing to do with investment banking. I've realized how much time I could have saved if I had done my research properly. This is why the research phase is the first in this process.

To excel in finance recruiting, you first need to know what it is. Finance, Wall Street, and markets are all buzz words tossed around. They can be confusing to those who've just started to be interested in the field. Research is key to not only understanding these words and concepts but also figuring out what you want to do.

WHAT ROLES ARE THERE WITHIN FINANCE?

As the main focus of this chapter is to give you the tools and methods for figuring out details for yourself, I won't cover the details of each job. I will, however, introduce the popular career choices of undergraduates. I'll provide bullet point summaries of different types of firms like investment banks, asset managers, hedge funds, and private equity. Detailed information regarding each role is available in many published books like *Vault Guide*.

Investment banks are financial institutions like Goldman Sachs, J.P. Morgan, and Morgan Stanley that perform a variety of different services. Within an investment bank are three different offices: front office, middle office, and back office. The front office has roles directly related to the firm's revenue generation. It provides the main services of an investment bank to its clients. The middle office has roles that aren't directly related to services or products that generate revenue for the firm but do work that supports the front office. The back office has roles like tech, compliance, and legal that support the logistics of the bank.

The front office is usually divided into investment banking and sales and trading. You may ask why there is a subcategory of investment banking within an investment bank. I've asked that question myself to many bankers and haven't yet received an answer better than "that's how people framed it." Investment banking is providing financial advice to clients in relation to capital markets, whether it be restructuring the capital structure or valuating a merger deal. Investment bankers provide advice on financial decisions clients need to make.

Within investment banking there are product groups and industry groups. Product groups usually include groups like M&A and Leveraged Finance whereas industry groups have healthcare, transportation, Technology, Media and Telecommunications, and Financial Institutions Group. How groups are divided generally differs by bank, but the aforementioned structure is most common. Typical work hours are very long and it is common to see people work more than 100 hours a week including weekends.

Sales and trading is another major component of front office at an investment bank. I like to think of it as the bulb of finance. It's the job portrayed in movies like *The Wolf of Wall Street*, *The Big Short*, or *Wall Street*. You may be familiar with scenes of huge floors filled with computers, monitors with complex graphs and texts and phones ringing here and there. The trading floor is depicted as a loud and energetic playground where people sit in chairs making money. The group includes different subgroups like sales, trading, research, and structuring. We can subdivide these groups into smaller units like equity, fixed income, currency, and commodities, but for the sake of this book, I'll only explain the bigger subgroups. The sales division manages client relationships, the trading division manages risk of the trading books, the research division conducts and publishes reports with professional opinion on behalf of the firm, and the structuring division creates complex derivative products for various needs. Unlike investment banking, work hours in sales and trading are relatively early because people have to be ready for action as soon as the market opens. However, when the market is closed, people are able to get off work much earlier than investment bankers.

Asset managers manage portfolios consisting of different assets and investments with purposes tailored to clients' needs. Hedge funds are specialized trading firms that trade sophisticated investors' money. Private equity firms specialize in investing equity that isn't marketed to the public.

Many other opportunities exist that I haven't discussed, like prop trading, quants, and risk management. I encourage you to put in the time and effort to read about the different roles in finance. You don't have to commit to the role you initially choose, but it's important you're aware of all the options available.

HOW TO FIND THE RIGHT ROLE

The most obvious way to figure out each role is to use Google. When you type "investment banking vs. sales and trading" or "What's private equity?" you'll find plenty of resources to help you draw a good outline of what each job entails. Make a small table like the one below with names of different roles and lay out the pros and cons of each.

	Investment Banking	Sales	Trading	Research	Asset Management	...
Description						
Pros						
Cons						

In the description, you want to fill in responsibilities, work hours, lifestyle, requirements, salaries, potential exit opportunities, and anything else you find relevant. Try to keep them succinct, preferably in bullet points. The goal here isn't to find the role that has nothing in the con section, but to create a table that can help to evaluate different roles and make an informed decision.

Unfortunately, Google doesn't tell you everything and, most likely, some of the information you'll find is wrong. So, the next step is to verify and dig in deeper by reaching out to people. You might not understand the roles completely and that's okay. The point of filling in the table is so that you've done your part before asking advice from professionals.

The information you get from these professionals is extremely valuable. You aren't going to stand out in an interview if all you know about the job is the information you found on Google.

Imagine you're on the other side of the interview, which is generally good practice in preparation for any job. You ask, "What's sales and trading?" One candidate answers, "It's a role where you buy and sell securities," and another answers, "After talking to Josh Jen and Michael Tan from your firm, I learned that sales and trading can be summarized as market making and risk management. They make a market for different securities for the client and also manage the risk of the book." With all other conditions equal, it's pretty obvious who you want to choose: the latter.

Both answers are correct, but we tend to favor the second person because the candidate's answer showed more effort. The candidate's answer wasn't only an answer to the question itself, but a demonstration of their interest in the job and the effort they took to reach out and learn more about it.

The key here, as you can see, is networking (discussed in Chapter 5). Networking is inevitably what you'll be doing after you're done with your preliminary research. You'll be asking different people with different backgrounds a prepared set of questions.

Who should you reach out to first? If you happen to have a family member or friend in the finance industry, go to them. Relationships and connections are extremely crucial in the finance industry and it's completely normal to ask for a favor from a family member or a friend. Try to utilize these connections first because they'll be your strongest network. If you're lucky enough to have existing connections, take advantage of them.

Not everyone has friends or family in finance. I didn't have any either. The next best choice is to reach out to alumni and upperclassmen at your institution. You might happen to know someone from a club in school or you might have taken a class with someone. Don't be afraid. Send them a Facebook message or an email and ask if they can help. Just like familial connections, school connections are extremely important. For instance, juniors or seniors who just finished their internships in the summer can be helpful. While senior professionals may not recall their internship experiences vividly, junior professionals can talk about their internship experiences in detail.

Repeat this process until you get a strong understanding of each role. Take notes in your table as you accumulate information.

THE IMPORTANCE OF DECIDING ON A ROLE

Now that you have a better understanding of the finance industry and the different and roles available to you, you need to decide on a role you want to pursue a career in.

You might want to apply to multiple roles, maybe to both investment banking positions and to sales and trading positions. Unfortunately, you're going to have to choose one as each role entails different responsibilities. While it's possible to apply to multiple roles, having more than two roles in your mind indicates that you still haven't figured out what you really want in a career. Applying to multiple roles inevitably requires a split of concentration and effort throughout your recruitment process.

KEYS TO BECOMING A FIEND

- Research is key: put in the time and the effort to read about the different roles in finance.
- Think in the interviewers' shoes.
- Create a table: laying out the descriptions, pros, and cons will help you make informed decisions.
- Verify the information you find online with professionals.
- Networking is key: family and friends, school connections, and LinkedIn are all helpful.
- Figure out what jobs you want to apply to.

CHAPTER 3

WRITING
A RESUME

It's easy to belittle the significance of a resume, but it's also easy to overthink it. I have seen the whole spectrum, from those who have typos and formatting issues with unclear bullet points in their resumes to those who spend days figuring out the words to use in a bullet point.

WHAT IS A RESUME?

Think of your resume as your face. Whether you like it or not, your resume will become your first impression to many people you meet throughout your career. It will define you, at least for the initial stage, throughout your recruiting process. It's meant to be an effective summary of who you are and it's your opportunity to argue why you're a great candidate for the job.

What kind of first impression do you want to make? Do you want to be seen as a charismatic leader? A passionate activist?

A diligent student? You should draft a resume that's right for you; so, tailor it to who you are.

WHAT SHOULD A RESUME LOOK LIKE?

First, download a resume template. It's important to refer to a template as each industry has different expectations. A finance resume, for example, drastically differs from an arts resume or a computer science resume. Some industries prefer to see creativity, whereas some, like finance, prefer order and uniformity.

If you don't have a template or you're uncertain if you're using a finance template, you can visit theundergraduate-fiend.home.blog and download one. It probably is one of the blandest resumes out there, but it's simple and familiar to the eyes of the professionals in the field, allowing them to easily navigate through your resume.

DRAFTING A RESUME: HEADER

No ideal resume exists, but you can compose a proper one. No resume will get you the job, but some resumes will cost you one. Refer to this resume when reading the following chapter for some context and example:

Chiwan Kim

2616 xxxxx xxxx Apt. xxxx, Durham, North Carolina, United States
(xxx)-xxx-xxxx | chiwan.kim@duke.edu

EDUCATION

Duke University Trinity College, Durham, NC — Graduation: May 2020
B.S. in Statistics, Concentration in Data Science, & B.S. in Economics, Concentration in Finance
- Cumulative GPA: **/4.0
- Relevant Coursework: Financial Derivatives & Engineering, ...
- Honors: Dean's List with Distinction - Fall`xx, Fall`xx, Fall'xx

Duke in New York - Financial Markets & Institutions, New York City, NY — January 2018 – April 2018
- Selected within 16 sophomore students for ....

Cheongshim International Academy High School, Gapyeong, Korea — Graduation: March 2014
- GPA: **/5.0, SAT 1: ****/2400 - Critical Reading ***, Math ***, Writing ***

WORK EXPERIENCE

JP Morgan, New York, NY – *Credit Trading Intern* — June 2019 – August 2019
- Pitched weekly credit trade ideas ....
- Created a template for profiling ....

Coolidge Corner Investments, Seoul, Korea – *Business Analyst* — June 2018 – July 2018
- Conducted market research ....
- Wrote a whitepaper for an ICO ....

Boston Consulting Group (BCG), Seoul, Korea - *Research Assistant* — June 2017 – August 2017
- Proposed strategic ideas and solutions ....
- Analyzed the cost and benefit factors of ....

MILITARY & LEADERSHIP EXPERIENCE

Republic of Korea Army, Pocheon, Korea - *Infantry Squad Leader / HR Administrative Sergeant* — August 2015 – May 2017
- Performed in three US-ROK combined operations ....
- Organized and managed 120 personnel ....

EXTRACURRICULAR ACTIVITIES

BSchool Program at Duke, Durham, NC – *Vice President* — August 2018 – Present
- Originated the content and wrote ....
- Co-organized and supervised weekly ....

...... union, Durham, NC – *Financial Analyst* — August 2018 – May 2019
- Managed the budget for ....
- Published the Duke Annual Report with ....

Duke Korean Undergraduate Student Association, Durham, NC - *Event Host / Emcee* — January 2015 – Present
- Hosted Korean cultural and entertainment events ....
- Wrote lyrics and recorded rap to ....

SKILLS & INTERESTS

- Languages: Native in Korean & English, Basic in Chinese (HSK level5)
- Technical Skills: Bloomberg Market Concepts Certification, R, Python, Tableau, Stata, and VBA
- Interests: Writing & Recording/Performing Rap, Book Writing, Escape Rooms

Write your name in bold letters in a large font size, followed by your current address, phone number, and school email in a small font size on the next line. Some people have asked me if they should change their names to a more "American" name. My answer is no. I have seen people who made up new names thinking recruiters would choose people with more familiar names. It's really important that you be yourself at all times throughout the recruiting process, whether it be on paper or in person. If you fake your way into the firm, the firm most likely won't be a good fit for you.

DRAFTING A RESUME: EDUCATION

"What's your name and what school are you from?" Frankly, this is the first question people often ask each other in finance networking sessions. People are interested in your educational background: your school, major, and GPA.

Two types of schools exist when it comes to finance recruiting: target schools and non-target schools. How do you know if your school is a target school? If firms come down to your school to present and hold information sessions for recruitment, you're probably a target school. This isn't always the case, but it's the easiest way to tell. Target schools tend to have a separate recruiting team within the firm, usually consisting of school alumni, meaning you'll be competing with your peers at school until the second round. But if you aren't attending a target school, you'll be competing with candidates also from non-target schools. Although candidates attending target schools are given a better environment and resources to work in and with, these candidates are not necessarily more likely to be recruited. Schools matter less than your edge. Everything really depends on you.

Next is your major or intended major. If you have more than one major or any additional certifications, make sure to write them on your resume as well. While it's statistically true that most professionals on Wall Street are economics majors, you don't need to be one. As long as you show passion and interest in finance and the field, your major shouldn't matter. Don't force yourself to be an economics or finance major. Study what you want to study.

Under your major, list your cumulative GPA, related course works, and any honors. Cumulative GPA should be self-explanatory as the number is provided on your most up-to-date transcript. Generally, you can round up to the first decimal point. If your GPA is 3.551, you can round it up to 3.6. Don't report over two decimal points or try to round up in some creative way. HR will most likely find out if you're doing so. Most firms on Wall Street have an official GPA cut of 3.2 out of a 4.0 scale. While 3.2 is the official cut, many people think of the cut as a 3.5, but this doesn't mean you cannot get the job if you're under 3.5. The point is, if you have a GPA over 3.5, you don't have anything to worry about. Lastly, regarding your major GPA, you might consider GPA omission. I've heard some mixed opinions, but most professionals I've consulted told me to report your GPA even if you aren't proud of it because firms will expect the worst if you don't provide it on your resume.

Next is your graduation year. Some people like to write "expected graduation," but I later learned from John Caccavale, a former J.P. Morgan trader, that this isn't recommended, as you're implying you may not graduate soon.

Next is your relevant coursework. Try to think of courses you've taken so far that are relevant to finance in any ways, like economics and finance courses. If you don't have any finance-related course work, add any course that is arguably relevant like probability or logic. Your listed courses, which can include those you're currently enrolled in, don't need to be finance courses as long as you can relate the content you have learned from the class to the roles for which you're applying.

Also, add honors if you have any. If you were on the dean's list or if you have any scholarships, this is the place to put them down. If you have any study abroad programs, scholarship programs, or exchange student experiences, put them below your primary education. Add a brief description of what the program was in no more than a bullet point.

Finally, add the name of your high school, your GPA, and your SAT/ACT scores—the only relevant high school information. This is the only part of your resume where you'll mention things that happened before college. Employers are looking to hire adults, not high school students. They don't care about what you've done in high school because they usually assume these experiences are trivial compared to what you've done in college as an adult.

DRAFTING A RESUME: WORK EXPERIENCE

Each work experience should include the name of employer, city and country where work took place, and the name of the position. Your work experiences should be in reverse chronological order, not by order of significance. For each work experience, restrict yourself to two bullet points. These bullet points should be about how you added value to the company during your employment and, if possible, followed up with what you were able to achieve. Below is an example:

Performed in three US-ROK combined operations as a squad leader/interpreter and participated in a total of 29 combat exercises; Recognized with three commendation awards for outstanding contribution and performance

The above example lists the work I did and the tangible results. Results can be an increase in revenue, sales, marketability, or anything relevant to the experience. If you're unsure, ask your boss or employer if any noteworthy enhancement occurred during your stay. You may not be fully credited for that improvement, but at least you can say you contributed to it. As such, you should always try to quantify your experience. Don't make up numbers, but using numbers allows potential employers to gain a better grasp of your work. Instead of writing "confronted customers on a daily basis," write "confronted 50+ customers daily."

Limit your bullet points to two and keep each bullet within two lines. All of them should start with an action verb, which are available on my blog *theundergraduatefiend.home.blog*, and should be used without repetition within the resume. Action verbs, according to *dictionary.com*, are "typically single words that describe what a person or thing in a sentence does." Starting your bullet point with an action verb will make you sound more confident and assertive.

Ideally, you should have some sort of work experience for each summer. If you're recruiting for your junior internship, you should generally have one work experience each in your freshman and sophomore summers. This is an ideal case, so don't feel discouraged if you don't have them. If you don't have any work experiences to reference, you can find opportunities on campus during the semester working as a tutor, tour guide, or administrative assistant. Try to make use of these if you don't have at least two work experiences.

Notice how the section is called work experience, not finance experience or professional experience. I've seen many people stressed out because they were worried they lacked experience related to the finance industry when recruiting for finance. I can confidently tell you that the industry you worked in doesn't matter at all. If you have an internship at a financial institution before your junior internship, that's great, but it isn't much better than working at a café serving customers besides its demonstration of your interest in finance. The lessons learned and skillsets acquired are more important.

If you have any unique work experience that defines your leadership experience, like military service, keep that section separate and divide the "Leadership and Extracurricular Activities" into "[the experience you're referring to] and Leadership Experience" and "Extracurricular Activities." The definition of unique experience can be subjective, but I haven't yet seen a case other than military experience so far that falls under this category. The same rules about bullet points and descriptions apply here as for work experience.

DRAFTING A RESUME: EXTRACURRICULAR ACTIVITIES

Academics and work experiences are important, but so is balance. Apart from academics, companies want to know who you are as a person. You'll find many other candidates who have similar backgrounds in school, GPA, and work experience. The extracurricular section is your chance to distinguish yourself from the crowd and show who you really are.

Write all the different activities you're involved in, whether they be clubs, fraternities or sororities, volunteer work, or any other personal activity you would like to share with the recruiter. List them in order of your passion for them. Be honest with yourself and select a few activities you think define who you are outside of the classroom. Do so with one caveat, though. You want to include one or two activities that show your interest in finance. This can be finance clubs or business fraternities. You want to show your recruiter you're willing to use your free time to learn more about finance. Employers in the industry assume this to be a genuine show of curiosity in the industry.

I've also noticed people including organizations and clubs they were never really involved in on their resumes. If you're including an experience, you have to be at least comfortable describing how you added value to it and what you've learned through it. You can get away with it sometimes, but, trust me, people ask for validation of your experience and are able to find out the truth in interviews or by speaking to other people.

If you aren't heavily involved outside of school, ask yourself, "What do I do during my spare time?" Everyone has their own way of spending time. Some people participate in a structured project through an organization while others independently pursue their interests in unstructured forms. I personally wasn't heavily involved in school activities. I loved writing lyrics and recording music. I didn't have an official club, but that didn't mean I wasn't allowed to write it under my extracurricular activities. Give a name to the activity and describe it through bullet points just like you would for any other activity. Don't be ashamed of doing so. After all, this section is to show who you are, not what clubs you're in.

DRAFTING A RESUME: SKILLS & INTERESTS

This section consists of three parts and each is written in a line with a single bullet point: languages, technical skills, and interests. The formatting of this section is rather intuitive. You'll have the three rows followed by the related content.

In languages, write down all the languages you can speak, write, or read and make sure to indicate your proficiency level in parentheses. If you don't speak more than one language, you can get rid of this line.

In technical skills, write down any relevant certification or technical skills. Coding languages are generally a plus, so if you can code in certain languages, include them in this section. A lot of people also debate whether they should include Microsoft Office Suite. While some say this doesn't add any value, my rule of thumb is to write it down under technical skills only if you're better at it than the average person or if you have no other coding skill set. The only certifications and technical skills you want to avoid writing are ones that are completely irrelevant like an official scuba diving certification.

The interests section is my absolute favorite. In many of my interviews, I've talked more about the content in the interests section than any other information on the resume. Interviewers want to learn who you really are as a person. They want to know what your passions are and what makes you unique. In fact, most likely, you'll meet someone who shares similar interests. If so, you'll be able to see your interview change from a strict, formal interview to a casual conversation talking about your shared interests.

A few of my interests were writing and recording rap, scuba diving, and escape rooms. Some people say escape rooms make the resume seem unprofessional, but what's so unprofessional about escape rooms? I've visited more than fifty different escape rooms and I really enjoy the activity. I'm more than comfortable passionately talking about my experiences in escape rooms and that's what really matters. In one of my interviews, I also had someone ask me where my favorite diving spot is and we had a nice conversation on where to go for the best dives. The interests section is what brings randomness to your resume and where you can add the cherry on top of your character. Don't underestimate the power of the interests section. I've had senior managers at Goldman Sachs and J.P. Morgan tell me that this section is the first thing they look at on a resume. They assume all candidates are competent enough for the job after the resume screening. They want to find people who are a good fit for the team. This doesn't mean you should just make up your interests to have potential bonding opportunities with employers. People will be able to tell if you're truly passionate about something or not. You don't need to add sub-bullet points under this section. All you have to do is list them in a line.

IMPORTANT TIPS TO KEEP IN MIND

Do a final check. Your resume should be less than a page no matter what. If you're over a page, play around with the margins, line spacing, and font to fit all the information on a single page. If you're still over, look back at your bullet points to see if you can paraphrase them. If you have space remaining, go back to the start of this chapter and brainstorm what you want to add. In the worst case, you can adjust the margins by a bit to make it seem to fill the whole page.

Now that we have a grasp on how to write a resume, all we have to figure out is writing the content. If you're a freshman or sophomore in college, you have plenty of time to figure things out. Make a list of the holes in your resume and try to fill in the rest. Knowing what you're missing is extremely important because the earlier you notice, the better you can prepare.

Once your resume is ready, share it with your friends, professors, family, and anyone you trust. Ask for general comments, typos, grammatical errors, and more. Read other peoples' resumes as well. Ask yourself what you did better and what you did worse. Use the feedback and repeat this process until the day you submit your application. Updating your resume has no end, so take all the time you have to improve it.

Resume tailoring is also an important task. You'll notice that firms differ from one another in style, culture, and philosophy. You'll be able to learn about the firm's color and criteria for new employees by looking at their official websites or networking with people at the firm. The criteria for hiring are probably similar for most places as they'll share demand in personal traits of diligence, loyalty, passion, teamwork, and attention to detail. However, some firms might have a stronger emphasis on some characteristics over others and, in this case, you want to tailor your resume accordingly.

Tailoring is especially applicable to those who are applying to different roles at the same time. If you were to apply to both investment banking and sales and trading roles, you want to tailor it to the role. Sales and trading places huge emphasis on teamwork, as the role requires extensive interaction, whereas investment banking assigns more importance to diligence and attention to detail. A general rule of thumb is to look at the job description of the role to which you're applying. You'll notice certain buzzwords in the job description that point to the skill sets the employer is looking for. The best way to tailor your resume is to use the same buzzwords in your bullet points. Technology has allowed employers to now scan through resumes through a computer to sort out resumes that contain buzzwords from those that don't. This is why reusing the important words in the job description is the most direct and effective way to tailor your resume to different roles.

Lastly, lying on your resume can lead to serious consequences in your career and, trust me, you don't want that to happen. I know people who've claimed to work at a certain firm only to be confirmed as a fraud after a short phone call. You'll notice how banker A knows banker B and trader C knows trader D. The finance community is much smaller than one would expect. Relationships are built daily between firms and clients, competitors, coworkers, and networks. Recruiters talk with each other as well, so you have to be careful when you're talking with people in this industry. Another common lie or exaggeration on resumes is language level. For some reason, people try to boast their language capabilities when they aren't truly at that level. I've seen candidates claim they're fluent in a language like Chinese only to meet an interviewer who actually speaks the language asking questions in Chinese. Of course, he was barely able to speak that language to that level, which led to an immediate awkward pause during the interview, consequently resulting in a rejection letter. Sometimes, people accidentally exaggerate their experiences, so make sure you check the accuracy of your bullet points when you're reviewing your resume.

Related to problems with exaggerating, you want your resume to convey a good mixture of humbleness and arrogance. Being overly humble won't get you the job. You want to sell yourself, but being completely arrogant can be worse. I've seen several cases of people overly exaggerating their experiences. It's natural to want to inflate your achievements, but you need to understand that the employers evaluating your resume were once in your shoes and know exactly what you're trying to do. Even if you have the most prestigious internship for your freshman year, most likely, they'll simply think that you might have some family connections within the firm, nothing more. Your resume isn't the first resume recruiters will be reading. Recruiters read through hundreds and thousands of resumes and they know when a college student tries to over-impress. Once again, honesty is key to your bullet point descriptions.

KEYS TO BECOMING A FIEND

- No resume will get you the job, but some resumes will lose you the job.
- You should be able to confidently speak to each bullet point on your resume when asked.
- Limit your bullet points to two and make sure that the format is aligned.
- Keep it to a single page.
- Be honest with yourself and genuine with your resume.

CHAPTER 4

WRITING A COVER LETTER

—

Dear Recruitment Team,

I am writing to express my interest in the Market Analyst Program Internship for the summer of 2019. I am amazed by the different roles, responsibilities, and, most importantly, the culture at J.P. Morgan. The conversations I had helped me develop a passion for the markets and I firmly believe I am an excellent fit given my skill set, experiences, and interests. My unique experiences have provided me with the foundation to tackle the exciting challenges J.P. Morgan offers. Thank you for your consideration, and I look forward to discussing my qualifications with you and learning more about Morgan Stanley.

I was about to attach this cover letter to my application until a friend of mine gave me an inscrutable look and said, "Morgan

Stanley? Really?" I would have made a fool of myself if I had submitted the application.

A sudden ominous feeling swallowed me. My eyes darted and skipped as I desperately searched through all of my past files to see if I had made the same mistake on other letters. My eyes stared at the countless cover letters I had written. The irregular beating of my heart began to falter when I saw the name Morgan Stanley written on every cover letter.

That was my sophomore year. I didn't know how to do things correctly then, but I do now.

WHY WRITE A COVER LETTER?
The trick here is simple: resumes aren't enough.

The resume does a good job introducing who you are, but it neither fully captures who you are nor explains why you're interested in the role and the company to which you're applying. Employers often make cover letters optional, but this doesn't mean they're trying to mislead candidates. Some people do get the job without a cover letter, but why not use the extra opportunity to sell yourself when given the chance? There's no good reason not to do so. Think of a cover letter as an extra page to communicate why you want the job and why you'll be good at it.

Some employers hint that they require a cover letter simply to increase the barrier for applying. Employers are aware that applicants submit applications to almost every firm they can. If employers were to require a cover letter, the chances of receiving applicants who aren't serious will decrease. It acts like a filter, removing those who aren't committed.

At the same time, some employers take cover letters quite seriously. A cover letter is intended to introduce yourself in more detail and persuade the employer why you're a good fit for the position. You should summarize yourself in a paragraph, express your interest in the position, discuss relevant experiences and how they prove you're a good fit, and provide contact information along with a polite ending. As long as you have these down on a single page, you should be fine with your cover letter. Just as with your resume, no cover letter will get you a job, but some will cost you one.

I have attached my cover letter at the end of the chapter as a reference. You can also visit my blog to download a template.

DRAFTING A REUSABLE COVER LETTER

Cover letters are harder to draft than resumes, as they have to be tailored to the company to which you're applying. You cannot use the same cover letter for both Citibank and Credit Suisse. Both firm-specific and role-specific contents need to be changed in every letter.

Your goal is to create a template that minimizes your need to make modifications. The highlighted section in the sample cover letter indicates the content that should be tailored according to the role and company. Some of these changes can be as simple as switching the name of one firm to another, while some require more in-depth research related to the role or company.

THE OPENER

Keep in mind that a cover letter is a letter; you need to include your name, address, phone number, and email address at the top right corner of your letter, each on separate lines. This information should be identical to the information you provide on your resume.

Then indicate the date on the left, followed by the recipient of the letter (the name of the firm to which you're applying) in bold. Make sure you're using the full official name of the company instead of using an abbreviation or alternative nicknames the company has. Then add the address of the company, which is usually available online, on the following line.

You can start your letter many different ways, but try to keep it simple. "Dear [company's name] Recruitment Team." Some people write down the recruiters' names, but tailoring to single individuals may be inappropriate when, in reality, others might be reading it as well. Don't limit yourself to one person.

It should look like this:

Chiwan Kim
440 Chapel Drive, Durham, North Carolina
123-456-7890
chiwan.kim@duke.edu

November 22nd, 2019

J.P. Morgan
383 Madison Ave,
New York, NY 10017

Dear J.P. Morgan Recruitment Team,

THE INTRODUCTION

The first paragraph of your letter should be an introduction.

Introduce yourself with your year in college, name of school, and major or intended major. This can easily be done in a sentence. The following sentence should be about the specific role you're interested in. Every company has its own way of referring to specific role. You'll be able to figure this out by either browsing through each website or by talking to professionals. Sales and trading at Goldman Sachs, for example, is referred to as "Securities," whereas it's referred to as "Markets" at J.P. Morgan. So, use the exact wording of the role in the job description page. Then elaborate on why you're interested in the firm and the role specifically. You can do this in multiple ways, but the best is to drop names of people you've networked with. You can say you were drawn to the firm because of [a], [b], and [c] after talking with [name], [name], and [name]. It's better if you can name both junior and senior people at the firm to show you've been exposed to both perspectives. This also shows that you've done your research and tried to reach out to current employees.

Although I haven't yet discussed networking in-depth, you can see how important it is to start your networking game early. Even if you don't have names to drop, elaborate on why you're interested in the firm. It can be the culture, the people, the role, or any other interesting facts about the company that made you want to write this letter in the first place.

Then in the last sentence, tie in how you are a good fit for the firm based on your skillsets, experiences, and interests. Although you'll be further elaborating on this in the following paragraphs, you want to provide a smooth transition into the body paragraphs where you'll be offering detailed descriptions of your past experiences.

THE BODY

You'll usually have room for about two to three body paragraphs, which means you'll have to choose two to three experiences that best exemplify or validate your claim that you're a good fit for the role. This section doesn't have a strict format and I advise against following one. You can include information you weren't able to convey in the two bullet points on your resume. In these few paragraphs, you want to show your readers what you've accomplished and acquired through your experience and why these skills are relevant for the role to which you're applying. Each paragraph will take on one experience. Briefly describe what you've done during the experience, what you were able to learn from it, and why this relates back to your candidacy.

You don't have to be original in style. The cover letter isn't a college application where you need to show a good balance of creativity, originality, and personality. It's more about conveying information about yourself efficiently and effectively.

CONCLUDING REMARKS

Your last paragraph should start out with a sentence summarizing how your skillsets align with the required skillsets for the job. The rest of the paragraph should include any other information you feel is necessary. This additional information could be where you're currently residing, if not at school because of a study abroad program or for other personal reasons, or it could be about your study toward your CFA or CPA or other certifications relevant to the role. Refrain from adding random facts about yourself and make sure everything is relevant. Then politely end the letter with phrases like "Thank you for your consideration" or "I look forward to discussing my qualifications with you." Add your phone number and email to remind them that you're open to any questions regarding your candidacy. You can also thank them for their time and express that you're looking forward to learning more about the company.

As I mentioned earlier, a cover letter is a letter. As you start the letter with "Dear [company's name] Recruitment Team," it should properly end in a letter format. You can close your letter with either "Sincerely," "Best," or "Thanks." Whatever works best and is most comfortable for you.

KEYS TO BECOMING A FIEND

- Just as with your resume, the cover letter should be a page long.
- The suggested guideline isn't a fixed template; you can add and/or take out parts.
- Tailor each cover letter to the company and the role.
- Make sure you change *all* the words correctly.
- Minimize the content needed to be replaced for each letter while maximizing the quality of the letter.

CHAPTER 5

WHAT IS NETWORKING? THE ULTIMATE QUESTION THAT NO ONE EVER ANSWERS

———

"How has the industry and your role changed as a result of the 2008 financial crisis?"

"Well, I wouldn't know. I started working in 2012."

Kevin definitely found a way to stand out among the crowd.

At a multifirm networking event, Kevin ran into an analyst at J.P. Morgan who mentioned he began working in 2006. He made a mental note and tried to ask a question that would set himself apart from most people who ask mundane questions. But when he asked the question, the trader from Bank of America looked at him funny. Kevin, being extremely sleep deprived, only then realized he was in a conversation with a different person. After this particularly mortifying experience, he now sticks to questions like "what type of sports do you like to watch?"

Networking is one of those buzzwords that consistently come up. It's a very simple skillset. Investopedia, a professional website focused on investing and finance education, explains it as "the exchange of information and ideas among people with a common profession or special interest, usually in an informal social setting." Once you start this process, you'll notice that it's easier said than done.

You need answers to many simple but difficult questions related to networking such as:

- Whom do I reach out to?
- What do I write in a reach-out email and how do I write one?
- When is the best time to reach out to people?
- What questions do I ask when I meet someone in person?
- How explicitly should I try to present myself?

Not all of us have family and friends we can ask these questions and get answers. I don't and I know plenty of others don't.

THE LUCKY 7

Networking is no doubt becoming more important and crucial to finance recruiting as the process starts earlier every year. Everyone has similar academic backgrounds, work experiences, and extracurricular activities, and it's hard to blame the candidates, given the limited time they had as a sophomore. Therefore, networking is an important tool that can be the game changer.

We can see how seriously companies regard networking by observing some statistics on new hires. Only 7% of all job applicants (not restricted to finance) have received a referral from an employee, but 40% of the hires were referred applicants. Even though applicants with a referral are a minority in the application pool, almost half of hires come from this group.

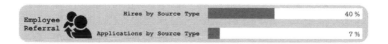

Many companies have referral bonuses. When a candidate the employee has referred gets employed, the employee receives a referral bonus. The company compensates the referrer for allowing the company to skip the preliminary assessments required. Given all this, it only makes sense that you want to be in that 7%. The odds explicitly work in that group's favor. Although preferable, you don't need to be officially referred by an employee. Strong relationship with employees conveys a similar effect.

FORMS OF NETWORKING

Networking comes in various forms. You can have non-personal interactions in the form of info-sessions and firm-related events and personal interactions in the form of email, phone, coffee chats, or site visits. Each method of networking is effective in its own way.

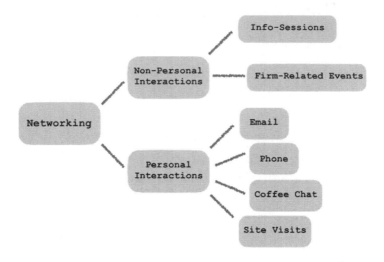

A NETWORKING LIST

You'll be connecting with a ton of people throughout the process. Even after you get your offer, your networking effort should continue, whether it be for team placement, internal mobility, or potential career transitions. Anticipate a massive list of people who can all serve as valuable networks. You want to remember the conversations you had with each person and some important details you shared with them. Networking isn't a one-time-only act. I can assure you that you'll be networking with people you've already networked with in the past, which is why an Excel sheet that contains all the relevant information is necessary.

You cannot remember the names, contact information, and details of the conversations you had with hundreds of people. I, for example, networked with 143 people in four months. How do I know this? I created an Excel sheet that organizes all the networks I've established throughout my recruiting process. I update this sheet to this day as I meet more people.

Your networking list should include any person you've talked to or will talk to in-person or remotely via phone, text, or e-mail. The more effort you put into completing this sheet, the more skilled at networking you'll be. Making a networking sheet isn't difficult and I assure you it will be helpful. The longer and more detailed the sheet, the more you can get out of it.

HOW TO CREATE YOUR NETWORKING LIST

Last Updated: 2020.02.04

Name	Company	Group/Team	Role	E-mail	Relevant Information	ROA	1st Networking	2nd Networking
Ryan Peters	JP Morgan	Equity Derivatives Trading	Analyst	ryan.peters@jpmorgan.com	Had a conversation about cooking, willing to actively help me out, joined the team 3 months ago, used to work in the sports industry	1	Phone	Coffee Chat
Willard Hampton/Will	Citibank	M&A Investment Banking	MD	will.hampton@citi.com	A school alumni, conversation did not go so well, talked about the investment club at school	2	Phone	Phone

This is an example of what your networking list should look like. Make a table with columns "Name," "Company," "Group/ Team," "Role," "Email," "Relevant Information," "ROA (Reach Out Attempt)," "1st Networking," and "2nd Networking" in this order. Most of these labels should be intuitive.

I personally bold the names of people with whom I feel strongly connected. I write the name they go by on the sheet if applicable.

In the "Role" column, write the title of the job and distinguish junior professionals from senior professionals. The roles are typically Analyst, Associate, Vice President (VP), Executive Director (ED), or Managing Director (MD) for many investment banks. This is important, as the questions you ask will depend largely on their roles. You don't want to ask questions like "what does your typical day at work look like?" to senior professionals because your immediate job isn't going to be relevant to what they do as managers. The question would be better asked to more junior professionals.

In the "Relevant Information" column, take notes on important information about the person or the conversations you had. You can write down mutual friends, the topic of your last conversation, and your impression. If you were introduced to another investment banker in the firm after talking to one, indicate that in this section. Write, "Introduced by [name of person who introduced them]." Generally, this section is solely for you to use to recall information about the person when you need to reach out. The more you write down, the better you'll remember.

In the "Reach Out Attempt" column, indicate the number of times you've attempted to connect. You may have reached out several times but received no reply. This is absolutely normal and I'll discuss this later on in the chapter, but, for now, we'll use this column to tally the number of times you've reached out.

The "1st Networking" column is to note the form of your initial networking activity. If you made a phone call, write, "Phone." If you had a coffee chat, write, "Coffee Chat." The "2nd Networking" column is to note the form of your follow-up networking activity. It can be identical to your first or different.

KEYS TO BECOMING A FIEND
- Understand the different forms of networking.
- Make a detailed fiend list and *actively* utilize it.

CHAPTER 6

INFO-SESSIONS & LINKEDIN NETWORKING

"I'm interested in *Running Man* (a Korean variety show)."

The managing director was probably expecting something more like "trading" or "banking" when he asked, "what are you interested in?" But Josh answered the question in his own way and, almost certainly, in the wrong way.

The managing director blinked a few times and the deafening silence filled their conversation. He had no idea what *Running Man* was and the conversation was instantly put to an end when another student came to break the silence and introduced himself to the managing director.

Networking is hard and requires practice to master.

INFO-SESSION NETWORKING

Info-sessions, short for information sessions that firms have on campus, are generally open to anyone without prior connections to the firm. While info-sessions are held throughout the academic year, they mostly occur right before the recruiting season in late August and September. Other firm-related events may occur as well. An alumnus might come into your class to talk briefly about their experience or an event may take place near your school. Take advantage of any event where you'll get the chance to network with people.

Info-sessions are usually the first form of networking activities, especially if you're a student from a target school. Firms may come to campus to give small presentations and offer networking opportunities with the people at the firm, depending on the school you go to. If your school doesn't have info-sessions, don't worry. The trend is changing, and many companies are trying to equalize the candidate pool by getting rid of the concept of target schools.

I strongly advise you to attend all the info-sessions that happen on campus. These events are generally searchable either on the school calendar or on the section of the firm's website that promotes on-campus events. As some firms make their info-sessions exclusive to certain years or limit the number or type of people, make sure you read the particulars. One time, for instance, I signed up for an info-session exclusively for women. I was among the first few people to arrive at the event, so it took me a while to realize I was the only man in the room.

Most info-sessions, if not explicitly stated otherwise, will require business or business casual attire. So be ready!

WHAT SHOULD I DO AT AN INFO-SESSION?

Here are the main goals for attending an info-session:

- Gain information you couldn't find online by asking questions or listening to their presentations
- Receive contact information from people at the firm so that you can start networking

I was walking in circles, not knowing what to do when I attended my first info-session. People jump out of their seats and surround the poor man in the suit, eager to steal the attention of the employee in hopes he'll remember them. The uncomfortable truth is that he won't. It's hard to expect the presenter to remember every attendee if they talked to multiple people, sometimes without name tags, simultaneously.

Treat info-sessions as primarily info-sessions. You don't have to impress people while you're there. In fact, if you try too hard, you might leave a bad impression that seeps into the memory of the employee.

QUESTIONS FOR THE INFO-SESSION

One managing director at Bank of America once told me a student asked, "What's your opinion on the current trend in interest rates? How do you think it will change in the next few years?" Sure, it's a good question to ask on the job, but really? The managing director said he really wanted to just start grilling the kid. Another managing director at Goldman Sachs had a student ask, "What keeps you up at night?" Do you *really* want to ask that question to a managing director?

The managing director wanted to ask, "Why are you interested in what keeps me up at night?"

The point is, you want to be genuine in all your comments and questions during any type of networking. Sit down and write questions you really want to know the answers to, the ones that you weren't able to find online. The information, examples, anecdotes, and answers you accumulate from professionals will allow you to indirectly experience life on Wall Street, which will give you a huge advantage in interviews.

Don't be embarrassed to ask simple questions like, "What are the different skill sets needed for investment banking and sales and trading?" The questions you might want to avoid are those that are personal like, "What's your salary?"

CONTACT INFORMATION

One tip: try to stay after the event.

Most people leave before the event is over. If you're one of the few who stays until the end, you have a better chance of having a more personal interaction. Often, I was one of the last people to stand with a list of questions I wanted answers to. Many willingly took out their business cards, allowing me to reach out in the future for follow-ups. Many of my connections began like this. Don't be afraid to ask for business cards or contact information.

If you do receive contact information, add it to your fiend list and follow up as soon as you can. If the event ends at a reasonable time during the day, follow up that day with a short email to thank them for their time and their answers to your questions. If the event ends later in the day, follow up the next morning. Try to include one or two sentences about the conversation you had with that person, perhaps something you bonded over. This increases the likelihood of them remembering you.

You now have built your first connection with the firm.

LINKEDIN NETWORKING

LinkedIn should be your next step in networking. This method is accessible to anyone who doesn't have great prior connections. This step is rather simple because it's more of a search tool than a reach-out tool.

First, create a profile that provides a brief introduction of who you are. It can include nationality, school, or any other information that can create some kind of common interest. Connect with immediate friends and family. Once you start searching for different firms, you'll notice that LinkedIn does a terrific job of suggesting profiles that might be relevant to you. If you were to search Citibank, for example, you'll be able to find a list of Citibank employees who have a shared background with you, like your school, club activities, or location. Then select a few profiles and write their contact information on your fiend list.

Many companies have a unified email address. So, we can make an educated guess of someone's email. If you find a person named Shirley Davidson from J.P. Morgan, you can assume her email is shirley.davidson@jpmorgan.com.

Sometimes, the email doesn't work, but it's still worth a try. Repeat this process and extend your fiend list so that you have at least one person from each company you're interested in.

Don't be upset if people don't respond. You're probably not the only one who didn't receive a response. One time, I was shadowing a salesperson at J.P. Morgan and noticed that emails were flying into her inbox almost every 30 seconds. But most importantly, make sure you're polite and show strong passion and interest in the role and industry in your message.

KEYS TO BECOMING A FIEND

- Take advantage of every networking event.
- Don't forget your main goals for attending an info-session: gain information you couldn't find online and get contact information.
- Refrain from trying to prove yourself at info-sessions.
- Ask appropriate and genuine questions when interacting with professionals.
- Be early or stay until the end of info-sessions to have more private interactions.
- Use LinkedIn more as a search tool than a reach-out tool.

CHAPTER 7

EMAIL NETWORKING

EMAIL NETWORKING

Email networking is the number one method you'll be using while networking. This method should be simple, but the way you do it can really make a difference. According to HubSpot, a company that creates platforms to grow businesses, 86% of business professionals prefer to use email when communicating for business purposes. This means that the professionals you want to be networking with are checking their emails more than fifteen times a day. This is why knowing how to effectively network via email is crucial.

You can send two types of emails: initial emails and follow-up emails. Initial emails will include a greeting, a brief introduction, an explanation of why you're reaching out, and a closing. These emails will mainly be directed to those whom you found through LinkedIn or were introduced to. Follow-up emails will include an expression of gratitude for the past interaction and possibly a request for more suggestions, advice, or additional contacts. These emails will mainly be directed to those you've met before and had a short conversation or interaction with.

INITIAL EMAILS

Initial emails are also known as cold emailing. Response rates for these emails are generally lower than your follow-ups. If you don't have any connections or haven't had interactions at an info-session or a firm-related event, this is your go-to method. You should browse through your fiend list, which should have names and contacts of people from personal, info-session, and LinkedIn networking, and send an email to a person of your choice.

Always write your email from scratch. Don't try to copy and paste emails you sent before when sending out new emails as you might for cover letters. The chances of employees figuring out you've been copying and pasting your networking emails are very slim; however, if you were to get caught, you would face serious consequences. Pretty much every company internally discusses their candidates when recruiting season comes. So, most likely, you'll become the topic of discussion. You don't want to be the person who spammed multiple people at the firm with the same email. You want to be the person who genuinely reached out to each individual showing at least the minimal effort of personalizing each email.

Your email should start with a direct and catchy subject, like "Reaching out from the 11/22 Info-Session_Chiwan Kim". This goes for all emails used for networking and it is much more effective to include your name in the subject line so they remember who you are whenever there is an update in the same email thread. The beginning of the actual email will start with a greeting along the lines of "Hi, [name]" or "Hello, [name]," instead of "Dear [name]," as it's more conversational. Then introduce yourself: your name, grade, school, and major or intended major. Tell them how you found their contact information and get straight to the main point of the email: *ask them for some time to talk*. Be polite and don't demand they give you their time. End your email with either "Thank you, [your name]" or "Best, [your name]." Unlike a professional cover letter, you want to be social and polite instead of stiff and awkward. It will come more naturally as you write more emails throughout the process, but always keep that in mind.

Below is an example of an initial email:

Hi, Ismael,

My name is Chiwan Kim and I am a senior at Duke University studying statistics and economics. I am interested in investment banking and recently found you on LinkedIn and noticed that you work in the investment banking division of UBS. If time allows, I would love to grab some time with you to ask few questions about the role and UBS in general.

Thank you.

Best,

Chiwan

THE FIRST FOLLOW-UP EMAIL

Follow-up emails aren't that different from initial ones, but you'll spend more time writing about the conversation you had earlier and expressing your gratitude for their time instead of redundantly introducing yourself. The conversation may have taken place at an info-session, site visit, coffee chat or through email, video conferencing, or phone call. Regardless of the form of your interaction, you need to follow-up with them.

The most important difference between the initial email and the follow-up email is, in the latter, you have to ask if they can direct you to other people whom you can reach out to at the firm. *This* is the most important step of networking.

Whenever you're networking with someone, your goal is to end up with two or more referrals at the firm. If you continue to do this, you'll see yourself drawing a huge tree of connections you've established at the firm. You will encounter cases when a person isn't cooperative but having this goal in mind will always push you to actively network. The network you establish *will* be the game changer.

Here's an example of a follow-up email:

Hi, Howard,

It was great talking with you today and I wanted to thank you again for making the time. I'm glad I was able to learn more about Foreign Exchange Sales at Deutsche Bank. Would you be able to direct me to few more people at the firm I can reach out to? I would love to get more exposure.

Thank you.

Best,

Chiwan

FOLLOW-UP EMAILS AFTER YOUR FIRST FOLLOW-UP EMAIL
You'll send multiple follow-up emails whenever you interact with someone, have another question, or have an update in your recruiting process. You'll send out more follow-up emails than initial emails.

One caveat to all this is to make sure you aren't too clingy. Use your fiend list to reach out to other people in case the person you reached out to is unresponsive. You should wait about two weeks for them to respond. If they don't respond within that time, send them another email on the same email chain and remind them you're still interested in talking with them.

Hopefully they'll reply, but if not, don't be upset. If they don't reply after this email, let them off the hook. Move on to the next person on your fiend list. The absence of a reply isn't an indicator of how much you're liked or not.

An example of the email would look like this:

Hi, Howard,

I just wanted to follow-up again to see if you can help me get more exposure to the firm. I'm really excited to learn more about the job and the experience at the firm and would love to talk to more people.

Thanks again!

Best,

Chiwan

KEYS TO BECOMING A FIEND

- Email networking is the most widely used form of networking, so utilize it.
- Understand the different styles of emails and their respective purposes.
- *Always* follow-up with an email.

CHAPTER 8

PHONE NETWORKING

This naturally leads us to the next phase of networking: phone calls. If people reply to your email, they usually offer a phone call to briefly chat. You don't want to sound unprepared and unprofessional. You want to be prepared with a list of questions.

QUESTIONS FOR THE PHONE CALL

Write down your objectives. It's your responsibility to ask thoughtful questions and connect with the person so they don't hang up and think they just wasted their time. It's important you keep yourself well-organized and efficient when asking your questions.

If I have a phone called planned with a current associate trader on the commodities desk at an investment bank, I would write down questions I want answers to before I make the call. Examples of these questions are, "What's the difference between an equity desk and other product desks?" or "How do I figure out if I have an interest in trading?" List questions you want answers to just as you would preparing for an info-session. While it's important to ask questions, keep in mind that you want to have a conversation with the person, not interview them.

If you're having a difficult time coming up with questions, take your time and carefully think about what you know and don't know about the firm. You may, for example, know what a trader does on the job, but might not have good understanding of when traders feel stressed.

Don't look up "things to ask in a networking call" on Google. These questions are overly used and, most likely, you won't sound genuine. If you're going to ask these questions, try to rephrase them in your own way. Instead of asking, "Can you walk me through your typical day?" be more specific and ask "I think I have a grasp of what the job mainly entails but I would love to learn the specific tasks on the desk. Can you give me a brief overview of what you're looking at during different times of the day?" The two ask the same thing, but the latter sounds more interested.

When the time comes to end the call, the same rule applies. *Ask if they can direct you to more people.* In any networking interaction you have, always ask this.

PREPARING FOR THE PHONE CALL
Hal Lin, a trader at Peak6, was waiting in a quiet lobby of a building for his phone call. He had planned a call at 5:00 p.m. only to be delayed for an indefinite amount of time. After waiting thirty minutes without an update, he decided to head back. On his subway ride home, the banker called, and Hal

picked up. The call started off on the wrong foot; they were barely able to hear each other. Hal quickly stepped off and ran outside to get better reception. But by the time he got out, the call was already a mess. Both of them were somewhat annoyed by the fact that they were wasting their time. Every response Hal received was shorter than the question he had asked and, consequently, the next ten minutes were very awkward.

You don't want to this to happen to you.

Sometimes, they'll initiate the call; at other times, you will. This should be clear on both ends; make sure a mutual understanding exists of who will initiate the call and the exact time. I had times when I wasn't sure who was calling whom for a prescheduled phone chat, which led to unintentional delays.

Sometimes, people run into unexpected events or simply forget. If you don't hear from them, keep calm and wait. The rule of thumb is to wait ten minutes after the agreed time, send an email asking if today is still a good time to talk, and let them know you're happy to reschedule if necessary. If they never get back to you, follow up after two weeks and see how that goes. If you still don't get a response, forget about it and focus on the other contacts you have on your fiend list.

But, on your end, don't be late and make sure you're in a quiet space where you have good reception. A lot of information will be thrown at you and you want to take notes during the call. You won't be able to remember the details of these conversations.

THE PHONE CALL

Assume each call has a fifteen-minute cap. This doesn't mean you should prepare only fifteen minutes worth of questions. Always be more than ready to talk for over thirty minutes. Sometimes they might have more time available, but if not, limit the conversations to few questions, or be in a hurry and offer to set up another call if necessary.

The conversation is broken down into greetings, introductions, and Q&As. It's an obvious breakdown, but I feel the need to explicitly state this to emphasize the importance of each phase. Start the conversation by checking the time they have to talk and letting them know you don't want to take up too much of their time if they're busy.

Don't rush this. It's more natural to start the conversation with a greeting and talking about the day or anything relevant. This can be a short conversation about life back at school if they're an alumnus, the weather, or activities during the weekend. You want to be more than just another eager applicant drilling them with a list of questions.

Once you're done with small talk, make the transition to your introduction, including your school, year, major, some bullet points on your resume you think are necessary to mention, and the field in finance you're interested in. Don't read your whole resume. Keep it concise and effective. You'll get to share more about yourself later on. This can be hard at times because it can come out awkward if you say "so… my name is…" Instead, go with something along the lines of:

"... By the way, thank you so much for your time today. I really appreciate your help. Well I think it's probably best for me to briefly tell you about myself before I start asking my questions. My name is Chiwan Kim and I'm a senior at Duke University studying statistics and economics. I served in the military in South Korea for about two years and served multiple roles throughout my service like driving tanks and conducting administrative work. Now, back at school, I've talked to a few people in the industry and have conducted my own research that led me to my interest in sales and trading, which is why I wanted to set up this call to learn more about it."

They'll probably talk about their own background after your introduction. See if they have a unique background that you can relate to or ask about. Remember, this is a conversation.

Now use your prepared list of questions. Prioritize questions that are most relevant to the person you're talking to. If I were talking to someone who works at a buy-side trading firm, I would ask questions like "Did you know you wanted to do buy-side trading?" or "What experiences prepared you for buy-side trading?" instead of a more general question like "What's the difference between sell-side trading and buy-side trading?"

Finally, end on a positive note. Thank them again for their valuable time and, most importantly, ask if they can direct you to more people at the firm. I cannot stress the importance of this enough. Make sure to follow-up with another email expressing your gratitude and your excitement about meeting more people at the firm.

Notice how all networking interactions are similar? It's a constant cycle of emails and phone calls. Many candidates aren't aware that networking can be approached systematically. Those who fail to recognize this complain that networking is bullshit and blame everything on the recruiting system without trying to improve their own networking skills. Networking is nothing more than establishing good relationships and a skillset that's necessary in pretty much any job.

KEYS TO BECOMING A FIEND

- Before your phone call, write down your objectives and the questions you want to ask.
- Prioritize questions that are especially relevant to the person you're talking to.
- Remember the phone call should be a conversation, not an interrogation.
- In any networking activity, ask if they can direct you to more people at the firm.

CHAPTER 9

COFFEE CHATS & SITE VISITS

COFFEE CHAT NETWORKING

You might have heard of what coffee chats are by now. Aside from the fact that coffee chats happen in-person, they're very similar to phone networking in the sense that the conversations are pretty much identical: a basic greeting and introduction followed by questions and a request for more contacts.

This networking activity is comparatively rare, especially if you aren't located in New York. This is a luxury enjoyed by those who can physically meet and have time to chat in person at a coffee house or even at the office, which might lead to site visits.

You might even want to schedule a trip to New York sometime and schedule a number of coffee chats in a week, as the effect of coffee chats is substantial compared to other forms of networking.

A request for a coffee chat might look like this:

Hi, Carroll,

My name is Chiwan Kim and I'm a senior studying statistics and economics at Duke University. I was directed to you by Tim after my conversation with him and was hoping to talk to you if you're available. I happen to be in New York from December 1 to December 5 so it'd be great if I could visit you over a cup of coffee sometime.

Hope to hear back from you soon!

Best,

Chiwan

GENERAL RULES FOR COFFEE CHATS

First, you absolutely don't need to drink coffee. You can drink whatever drink you want as long as it is non-alcoholic.

Secondly, professional attire is your safest bet; it's always better to be overdressed than underdressed. You are evaluated in any networking activity you participate in, so it makes sense to fully dress up, unless explicitly told not to.

Third, bring printed copies of your resume and some paper you can take notes on. I personally only take out my resume if they ask for it, but I see no problem with providing them with a physical copy if done in a natural way. I usually don't use the paper I bring because I memorize the questions I have to ask and I want the coffee chat be more conversational and natural.

Lastly, always be early, as nothing is worse than being late. John Caccavale, a retired J.P. Morgan trader, shared a story with me about a candidate who was immediately dismissed for being late to the interview. The candidate nearly begged for another chance, but there really was no reason to hire someone who was late to an interview. People in the finance industry are always busy and they take their time very seriously. There can be unexpected delays, so plan your trips with extra time as a cushion. Your counterpart may be late for unforeseen circumstances or for other reasons. Email them after ten minutes to check in and remind them you're waiting at the coffee shop just as you would for a phone call.

THE COFFEE CHAT

Having arrived early, you'll probably find yourself in an awkward position debating whether to order now or later. I've been in this situation countless times and it never gets better. My way of solving the problem was to send an email ten minutes before the meeting, asking if I could get them anything while I was waiting. This reminds them I'm waiting and is a polite gesture.

Now that you're in line ordering your drink, take this time to reintroduce yourself. It's always good to offer to buy the coffee since they're the ones doing you a favor.

Once you sit down, start asking the questions you had in mind while making sure you're having a conversation rather than interrogating them. If you ask someone about the different kinds of desks in trading, they might mention the word "FICC" in their explanation. If you don't know what "FICC" is, ask, even if it's not in the list of questions you've prepared. This seems obvious, but sometimes you don't act the way you intend to when you're nervous.

Keep track of time and remind them of the time when it approaches twenty minutes. People usually block out a thirty-minute time slot in their schedules for coffee chats, but sometimes they're in a hurry.

Once you're finished with your questions, ask if they can direct you to more people. You might worry you'll sound disrespectful, but you're not. They understand your situation, as they were in your shoes a few years back. You shouldn't ask for more contacts if they've already provided you with additional contacts or told you they weren't able to.

When the chat's over, use your time wisely by walking back with them to their firm. This will be your last chance to leave an impression, so make use of this time. More importantly, make sure to thank them again in your follow-up email once you get back home.

SITE VISIT NETWORKING

Site visits are the most effective form of networking and probably the most rewarding experiences you'll get in networking. These visits will give you first-hand exposure, the chance to meet different people, a picture of what a day at work looks like, and a sense of the culture of the firm. Just like coffee chats, site visits are a luxury for those who live near firms or who can visit.

Site visits can last from thirty minutes to multiple hours. If you're given the opportunity to visit the office, observe and absorb as much as you can. These experiences will allow you to respond to interview questions with detailed answers. Unfortunately, site visits tend to be more common for people interested in sales and trading than for people interested in investment banking or other parts of finance as they're on the private side and deal with confidential information.

THE SITE VISIT

Few people are given the opportunity to visit, but if you're lucky and invited, dress professionally, take notes, and bring copies of your resume.

Once you meet the host, thank them for the invite and express your excitement. The structure of site visits varies depending on the host, but most will try to help you by letting you sit with different people on the floor so that you can get the most out of the experience. You may be sent to different desks on a trading floor so you experience both sales and trading across different asset classes. Most importantly, make sure to get contact information as you sit with different desks.

You don't want to be that annoying kid. Be attentive to the situation so that you know when to ask questions. If you think it might be a bad time, don't ask.

Keep in mind that the people you shadow are doing their jobs. Let them know you're able to learn even by staring into the screens of their work. It's important you don't ask questions when they're busy. Awkward pauses here and there in your conversations are completely fine.

The questions you ask in a site visit should be more sophisticated than the ones you ask in a coffee chat or on a phone call. People generally expect more from you if you're at the firm. You look bad if you're asking the most basic questions like, "What is trading?" when you're sitting in the middle of the trading floor. You're most likely assumed to be a passionate candidate for the role and people might even try to grill you with questions related to the job. When I visited the Bank of America office to sit with an options trader, for instance, he didn't really explain what was going on at his desk or answer my questions. Instead, he asked me different brain teasers and technical questions about options just to see how competent I was. This is why a site visit can be a hit or a miss. You can effectively impress people and build very strong personal relationships by asking good questions and showing good personality or you can leave a horrible image if you ask the wrong questions and show bad character.

Just as in any other networking interactions, thank the host and send them a follow-up email expressing your gratitude. Also, make sure to follow-up with all the people you met at the site visit.

KEYS TO BECOMING A FIEND
- The general framework for preparing for coffee chats follows the framework for phone calls.
- Keep the conversation natural. It's not an interview.

- Be prepared with your resume at both coffee chats and site visits.
- Site visits can be a hit or a miss. Be fully prepared to ask good questions and show good character during your visit.
- Make sure to follow-up after each coffee chat and site visit.

CHAPTER 10

THE STEPS TO BECOMING A REAL FIEND

———

Networking is a habit. You need to be a fiend for it; you need to be able to comfortably network anywhere at any time. You'll run into people who matter and be given unexpected chances to create valuable networks. I, for instance, once ran into an associate at Morgan Stanley whom I had met at a firm-wide event at a bar in New York. This interaction led to another and, eventually, he and I got close enough for him to invite me to his office.

The key to getting better at networking is practice. It might take a lot of time to draft your first professional email, but you'll notice it gets easier with practice. The same goes for coffee chats and personal interactions. The more you do it, the better you'll get.

THE GATEWAY AND THE GUARDIAN

When it comes to networking, it's extremely important you find a gateway person and a guardian for each firm. The gateway person is going to be the first contact you establish with the firm, most likely the person who first gave you additional contacts to reach out to. Once you have your gateway person, branch off to create your massive tree of networks.

First, send out initial emails and go through the networking process I explained in earlier chapters. Then send a follow-up email asking if they can direct you to more people at the firm. Once they provide you with new contacts, they become your gateway person. It's extremely important to know who your gateway person is because every networking activity is, in essence, stemmed from them. Add this information to your fiend list and don't forget it.

Let's say you reach out to Nick Hibshman, an analyst on the Cross-Asset Structuring team at J.P. Morgan, who introduced you to two additional analysts, Man-Lin Hsiao, an analyst on the Macro Investable Indices team, and Shihab Malik, an analyst on the Corporate Derivative Marketing team. Treating Nick as your gateway person, you can write your initial emails to Man-Lin and Shihab mentioning that Nick told you to reach out.

Below is an example of an initial email:

> Hi, Man-Lin,
>
> My name is Chiwan Kim and I'm a senior at Duke University studying statistics and economics. I was referred to you by Nick after we talked on the phone

and would really appreciate it if we could connect sometime.

Thank you.

Best,

Chiwan

As recipients of emails like this, Man-Lin and Shihab will inevitably develop first impressions of you that are much better than an initial email without a name drop.

This is due to small nuances and psychology. First, Man-Lin and Shihab now know they were referred to you by Nick, so they feel responsible to help out. Secondly, the fact that Nick directed you to them makes them think you have already been approved by Nick, which serves as a strong plus. They would not think Nick would have introduced you to them if you weren't worth their time. A single familiar name in the email can be a game changer.

Now let's assume your conversations with Man-Lin and Shihab went well and you asked if they could introduce you to more people. Man-Lin directs you two more additional contacts of her own and Shihab does the same. You'll see the number of the contacts exponentially increase as you branch off from each network. Once you repeat this circuit, you'll be able to create a whole tree of independent relationships at the firm. After a few months of heavy networking, return to your gateway person with a follow-up email to let them know you've been able to meet Man-Lin, Shihab, and others and thank them for their help. This can strengthen your relationship with your gateway person.

Having ten or more branches at a single firm is a good indicator that you've done a quantitively sufficient amount of networking for that firm. Another important factor in this networking game is the depth of your network. The guardian will be the most supportive and helpful person at the firm and this may be your gateway person. The guardian is going to be the person who will strongly support you during internal discussions for candidacy and will be your go-to person whenever you're facing difficulties throughout the recruiting process. Review your fiend list and mark the person you're most comfortable with. It's better if they're a more senior person at the firm, as they're more involved in the selection process, but a junior person can also provide you with detailed insights and information if necessary.

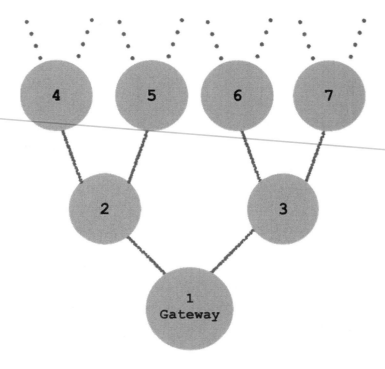

THE ONE-PERSON-ONE-FIRM RULE

First, line up nine to ten firms you want to join in order.

Second, break them down into tiers of your own so that you have your favorite three firms in tier 1, the next bundle in tier 2, and the rest in tier 3. When you allocate time and energy in networking, you want to put more weight on tier 1 and tier 2 firms than tier 3 firms.

Third, network with at least one person at each firm on the list. This can be as simple as having your initial emails sent out to start new conversations or having a phone call planned with someone at J.P. Morgan, a coffee chat planed with someone at Barclays, and emails exchanged with someone at Morgan Stanley. Whatever the form is, having an interaction with at least one person at each firm is an optimal number to hit at every point in time.

This is an effective method because you can expand your network at a fast rate and keep the big picture of the industry by consistently getting input from different institutions. Spotting similarities and differences between firms will be easier, which will help amend your preference list as you proceed with your networking.

I personally networked with one person from each firm at a time, as it allowed me to better focus on the existing relationship at a firm. I was able to ask more thoughtful questions each time and develop new ones for the next person I interacted with instead of asking the same question to multiple people.

FIENDS DON'T GIVE A FUCK ABOUT GOSSIPS

Some people say networking isn't that important. Many people are disgusted with the superficial talk and say networking is just kissing ass motivated by hidden intent. If you're surrounded by people in this group, it might be harder for you to actively network. You may be worried about people judging you for being a try-hard. I, too, had friends who made me feel like I was doing something wrong and embarrassing whenever I networked. Many times, I wondered if I was overdoing it. In the end, I decided that none of this mattered because reaching out to full-time employees to get some form of help is reasonable, whether it be for general advice or a direct referral.

The point is, you need to disregard all the noise, even if you're surrounded by those who are against networking. You need to keep up with what you've been doing. It's true that some people land their jobs without doing any networking, but I've seen more people land their jobs with the help of networking. Networking is important before, during, and after your internships and even after you return as a full-time employee.

I've included this section to highlight the importance of disregarding the gossip and peer pressure when it comes to recruiting. I've seen people worn out not because of recruiting preparation, but because of unnecessary stress from peer pressure. It's a long and stressful journey, and you should be proud and confident about all of your networking.

After all, what is there to be embarrassed about in building your own professional connections?

FINDING YOUR SWEET SPOT

After observing those who are good at networking, I noticed that highly skilled fiends are those who know their strengths. Networking becomes much easier once you figure out what your strengths are.

Take a moment to reflect on your relationships with friends and family. What are you known for? What's your character? If you're a fan of the TV series "Friends," you'll know Chandler is the funny one. Are you the funny one in your group? The smart one? Everyone has different characteristics that can be converted into strengths. Understanding your strengths becomes extremely helpful when you network.

If you're having trouble figuring out your strengths, ask your close friends, family, or someone with whom you speak frequently. Accumulate their opinions and decide on what your edge is. Then emphasize that character the next time you network. Companies are looking for people to work with, not robots.

I tend to be the more sincere and mature one in my friend group. I've heard multiple times from people I've networked with that they got the impression that I was mature after talking to me. Sometimes, they would even add that this naturally helps them believe I'm a responsible person who they can potentially work with in the future. Nick Hibshman, an analyst at J.P. Morgan, has a more sociable image and his strength is his humor. I would always see Nick making jokes when he networked with people, which is also a great character to have as a coworker.

Your style doesn't really matter as long as it's your most effective way to appeal to other people. After figuring out your appeal, remind yourself during your talks on the phone or coffee chats that you want the other person to see you in that light. People generally don't remember other people by their specific details but by impression. You should make an impression that truly represents you.

WORKAROUNDS FOR WEAKNESSES

Everyone has a weak spot. Even the top fiends have room for improvement, whether it be content, style, or delivery in networking . We already established the importance of knowing your strengths, but it's equally important to know your weaknesses.

Some people use their hands more actively when they're nervous and make all different kinds of unnecessary hand gestures when they communicate. Some people use the same word or phrase repeatedly to such an extent that it annoys people.

Thousands of other candidates are competing for the same dream job of working on Wall Street. Firms are aware of this as well. With plenty to choose from, it only takes one simple reason to shut your application down. Even your smallest habit might serve as a potential reason for not hiring you. Unfortunately, networking is a social skill and social skills matter tremendously in almost any career.

We want to prevent any chance of disqualification throughout the process. One of the best ways to find out your weaknesses is to ask close friends and family members who are comfortable enough to be frank with you. Just like how you asked around for your strengths, do the same for your weaknesses and you'll discover the different flaws you have in terms of presenting yourself. Another way is to practice speaking and introducing yourself in front of the mirror. You never really get the chance to look at yourself when you're talking, so it might be a good idea to see what you look like when you speak. You might be able to spot something you never realized you were doing, hopefully early enough that it hasn't yet hurt you throughout the process.

RECORDING INFORMATION

You might have already noticed how important it is to record the information you obtain from any networking. We don't want to forget information. We need it to ask more sophisticated questions. The more detailed the questions are, the more information you'll get that nobody else knows. These details you share in your interview will differentiate you from the crowd. Also, you might have to talk to the same person again in the future and you don't want to repeat your questions.

Recording information is much easier if you're networking on the phone or through email than at a coffee chat or site visit. In the latter cases, try to write down the main questions on a piece of paper before you jump into your networking event. After you're finished talking to the person, go back to your paper and fill in the answers for each question. It will be much easier to recollect your memory the sooner you write.

CONFIDENCE AND THE SMILE

Recruiters evaluate candidates from a homogenous pool, but you can stand out in the first few seconds with a smile, positive energy, and confidence. Of course, overdoing anything is problematic. Regardless, it's extremely important that you smile and show positive energy and confidence in any of your interactions.

First impressions are difficult to change, but if you start with a pleasant smile, you're bound to leave a positive impression. Who doesn't like a genuine smile and positive energy? Also, be sure to show you're confident from the start. This can even be achieved with a firm handshake, which was what Matt expected to see from me when we first met in the J.P. Morgan lobby. Grab the hand and shake it with a firm grip with enough strength that if the person were even a bit drowsy, you would wake them up. Once the conversation starts, smile when appropriate.

The whole point of this is to convey that you're excited to be there to talk about their personal experiences and learn more about the firm. These small gestures make a real difference in leaving a lasting impression.

TOO MUCH CAN BE POISON

You want to be a fiend, not a foe. A fine line exists between them that you don't want to cross. You don't want to be too much in anything. Put yourself in the shoes of the person on the opposite end. Will this question lead to an awkward conversation? Is this question offensive?

A few don'ts to keep in mind when networking:

Don't be inconsiderate of others' time. If you're on the phone with someone who was generous enough to help you out, make sure you aren't taking up too much of their time without some form of consent. It's always safe to ask how much time they have when the call starts. A rule of thumb is to keep the call under thirty minutes.

Don't network with too many people at the same firm at the same time. A colleague of mine was so determined to get an offer at one of the bulge bracket investment banks that he decided to send out emails to all the contacts he had for the firm. After he sent out ten initial emails to ten different people, he was told he shouldn't have done that. Firms have internal discussions on potential candidates, especially during recruiting season. You don't want to seem insincere.

THE POWER OF SOCIAL MEDIA

Companies have started to look at social media accounts of potential candidates to gather more information about them. A little creepy, right?

Social media is powerful; it's hard to find anyone without a Facebook, Instagram, or Snapchat account. Companies assume that what you put on social media is a more accurate depiction of who you are than what you display at an interview.

I've seen recruiting teams send Excel sheets with links to candidates' social media accounts to interviewers. You need to make sure you don't have inappropriate content online. While you don't have to restart your social media account, it's a good idea to censor some of the content you feel uncomfortable sharing with your interviewer.

NETWORKING OF A GOOSE

Have you ever noticed the V-formation geese fly in? Have you ever wondered why they fly in that way? Flying as a flock in this formation minimizes the air resistance for the geese in the back. If a goose cannot continue to fly, two other geese separate from the main flock to fly with the struggling goose, forming a smaller V-formation.

When I first heard this, I was fascinated. Geese remind me of the importance of social bonds and relationships, and I believe others value the importance of these as well. Acknowledging the power of personal relationships, friendships, and networking is key to success, in finance recruiting and in life in general.

KEYS TO BECOMING A FIEND

- Make networking and recording information a habit.
- Your guardian and gateway person are going to be your crutches throughout the recruiting journey.
- The "One-Person-One-Firm" rule is *key* to effective networking for your top ten choices.
- Don't get discouraged when other people talk badly about you; you're doing just fine.
- Know your strengths and weaknesses.
- Smile and show confidence.
- Too much is never good. Always keep in mind the thin line that makes a fiend into foe.
- Your online social media accounts are representative of you.

CHAPTER 11

STUDYING YOUR AREA OF INTEREST

———

In this chapter, I want to introduce you to prework necessary to prepare you for your interviews. The following content is applicable to any applicant within the finance industry regardless of the position they're looking into.

READING THE NEWS

You need to keep up with both domestic and international news on financial markets. Regardless of your track, it's difficult to argue that you're interested in finance when you have no clue what's going on in the financial markets. Every position in finance is relevant to the financial markets in one way or another. The earlier you subscribe to the *Wall Street Journal* or *Bloomberg News*, the faster you'll understand what's going on in the world and, more importantly, the finance world.

I understand people have busy schedules and some may find it difficult to read through different newspapers front to back.

At least read the headlines for each day so you're aware of what everyone else is talking about. In fact, I myself use *Bloomberg 5 Things to Start Your Day, Seeking Alpha's Wall Street Breakfast*, and *Yahoo's Finance Morning Brief* instead of reading the whole paper. These three offer summaries of important market news each day. I use all three in order to develop a broader understanding of different issues.

Reading finance news is hard. It takes time to read and understand, especially when you first start reading them; articles may use financial jargon you are not yet familiar with. Don't worry; it will come with practice. Important macro issues tend to repeat and as you continue to read the news, you'll soon be able to better grasp the concepts and subjects dealt with.

Once you get comfortable with reading the news briefings from *Bloomberg, Seeking Alpha* and *Yahoo Finance*, try to read relevant articles in the *Wall Street Journal*. It has a sub-scription fee, but I highly advise you subscribe to it, as it's one of the most highly used sources for news on the market by finance professionals.

DIGESTING MARKET NEWS

As you start reading through market news, you'll notice two categories: regular and spontaneous. Regular news is news that either appears routinely or consecutively over a short time, like Brexit, the U.S.-China trade wars, Fed rate cuts, and any other announcements of important macro data. Spontaneous news is news that appears as a one-time event, like the attack on oil pipes in Saudi Arabia, the announcement of a new cyber-truck by Elon Musk, and random tweets on the economy by President Donald Trump.

You should understand both types, since firms will expect you to have a good understanding of what's going on in the markets and test you during your interviews. While it's relatively easy to read up on spontaneous news when interviews come, regular news isn't crammable. This is why it's important to start reading the news now. The earlier you start, the better.

Let's say an article is published on the relieved tension in the U.S.-China trade wars. Someone who just started reading the news will naively assume the political situation has been alleviated, whereas someone who started reading a year earlier will recognize that it isn't the first time tension has been relieved. The point is, you'll know a topic much more in-depth when you're asked to give your opinion on specific news. With more color and context of the situation, you'll be able to support your opinion with evidence.

Consider an article on the Fed's decision to cut tax rates. Is this good for the economy? You would be clueless if you had no context on where Fed rates were initially and how influential this metric is to the rest of the market. If people say rates are rising at a concerning rate, are we at a historic high? As you accumulate more background information, you'll be able to better understand and critically interpret different news.

If you're behind or lacking information, the regular news category often has articles that offer summaries of each important phase of the event along with reasons why the event is relevant to the market. Ideally, you shouldn't need this, but they work in a pinch.

ORGANIZING NEWS

I created a chart like the one below to organize all the information, which was extremely effective whenever I had to share my knowledge or opinion on the markets.

	Equity	Fixed Income	Currencies	Commodities
Topic 1				
Topic 2				
Topic 3				
Topic 4				
Topic 5				
Topic 6				
Topic 7				
Topic 8				
Topic 9				

This chart allows you to have nine different news topics ready at all times. You should know these topics inside out and be able to explain each with your opinion on how the event impacts or will impact the financial market if someone asks.

The first three topics should be topics that frequently appear on the news and that most people, even outside of finance, are familiar with. Brexit news, for example, isn't limited to the finance industry. The next three topics should be topics that aren't headline news but are relevant to the financial market, like news on easing of bank restrictions, policies passed to stimulate the Chinese economy, and changes in political positions. The final three should be topics relevant to finance, but require active research and that only you might know of.

Full-time professionals and your potential interviewers won't always have the time to read through every single piece of news out there. So, this is your time to shine. Always have at least three topics professionals might not be aware of but that you personally find interesting and relevant to the financial markets. These can be specific to a company or related to one of your past experiences. Whatever they are, they will serve as a hidden card, especially when the interviewer is looking for more than just a basic understanding of financial markets.

In the columns section, you'll notice four different asset classes: Equity, Fixed Income, Currencies, and Commodities. Your job is to brainstorm how each topic will impact these asset classes and the market and determine which asset class will be most affected.

If you, for example, have a recent Fed rate cut as one of your nine topics, you might believe the equity market will appreciate as a result of an increase in overall market sentiment and investor confidence or, conversely, that it will depreciate as a result of growing fear in general market sentiment and investors reading into the Fed's decision as a warning to the current markets.

No right or wrong answer exists, but you need to choose at least one asset class and what you think will happen in the market as a result of your topic choice. If you believe the news will impact several markets, write your opinion for the corresponding columns with your rationale.

Make sure to keep your chart updated with numbers, statistics, and content as you read through your daily news. Also, feel free to replace a topic at any time. The point of this chart is for you to have nine different topics you can freely talk about. These nine topics will be your arsenal of knowledge you can always reach into.

KEYS TO BECOMING A FIEND
- Keep up with market news.
- Make reading the news a habit as soon as possible; it's a skill that comes with time.
- Use the framework above to organize your knowledge and opinion on the market at all times.

CHAPTER 12

PREPARING FOR THE INTERVIEW

Welcome to the last stage of your journey. Congratulations on making it this far. Receiving an opportunity to interview isn't easy and you should be proud of yourself. You're now very close to the end of the recruiting game. You need to keep a few important points in mind in this stage. If you've been closely following the directions provided in previous chapters, you're already well ahead of many other candidates.

DIFFERENT TYPES OF INTERVIEWS

Improvement in technology has led to rapid changes in finance recruiting. Many financial institutions have two to three interviews for those who pass initial resume screenings. Many companies have substituted their first interview with an online recorded interview, which is followed by a final interview, also known as "Superday." Superday interviews generally entail a couple of in-person interviews onsite and are interactive.

Interviews, therefore, can be divided into two broad categories: remote and in-person. Remote interviews usually take the form of phone or video, which can be pre-recorded or live, whereas in-person interviews happen onsite.

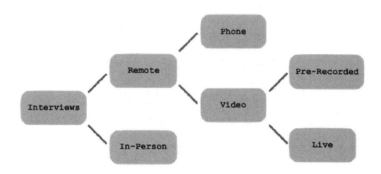

Regardless of the form the interview takes, all interviews consist of behavioral and technical questions. Behavioral questions are asked to assess the candidate's personality, beliefs, priorities, and character. This is essential to any interview because, in the end, they want to know if you're someone they want to work with. Technical questions are asked to assess the level of technical knowledge required for the job. While it's more common to see both types of questions in an interview, some firms only ask either behavioral or technical questions. As most jobs in finance require both technical knowledge and behavioral aptitude, your job is to be prepared for both types of questions.

BEHAVIORAL QUESTIONS

Most behavioral questions can be prepared. I'm not implying you'll be memorizing your answers for every possible interview question, but you can effectively brainstorm answers.

Below is a list of questions you can use for your framework. It covers the high-level points often touched upon an interview:

- Talk about yourself.
- Why finance?
- Why [name of division]?
- Why [company]?
- What's going on in the markets?
- Pitch a particular company you follow.
- What are your strengths and weaknesses?
- Talk about a time you exhibited leadership.
- Talk about a time you have been challenged.
- Talk about an experience that sets you up to succeed in [role].
- Variations of other behavioral questions
- Any questions for the interviewer?

When answering any behavioral questions, first provide a short and direct answer to the question, then follow with one or two relevant examples from your experience. If the question is, "What are your strengths?" your response should be, "My strengths are [A], [B], and [C]. I believe these are my strengths because... [examples]."

BEHAVIORAL QUESTIONS: CREATING AN INTERVIEW TEMPLATE

The interview template is essentially an idea bank with stories sourced from your experience. You can't predict and perfectly prepare every possible behavioral question, but you want to be ready. You'll be surprised by how one story can be used to answer many different questions, even ones you weren't directly prepared for, just by tweaking how you phrase it.

One of the stories in my idea bank is about the performance measuring mechanism I developed during my consulting internship. My team was having trouble measuring productivity of a sector within a client company because of the limited metrics the company had internally, but I was able to come up with a new metric using unexpected data. I initially prepared this story to answer the question, "Talk about a time when you were creative" by emphasizing how I was able to think creatively within the limited data source we had. But then, I noticed I could rephrase this story to answer questions like, "Talk about a time when you were challenged" and "What are your strengths?" In answering the first question, I placed more emphasis on how hard our team worked and how much the team struggled until I came up with a solution. In answering the second question, I identified creativity as my strength by emphasizing how innovative the metric I used was.

As you can see, a story from your idea bank can be applied to different questions as long as you smartly rephrase it. Try to come up with answers to the twelve questions listed above and at least two stories for each, with three stories for strengths and weaknesses. The more stories you have, the easier time you'll have answering questions on the spot. Try to come up with as many stories, examples, and ideas from your experiences as possible.

The fifteen stories in my idea bank were enough for all the interviews I had. The template takes care of most of the content needed for any behavioral questions. It will take time to make, but will apply to any interview you have in the future. Make sure you know your stories inside and out.

I've indicated some key points to keep in mind when creating your stories for the listed questions:

1. Talk about yourself
- Keep your response under 50 seconds.
- Include your name, school, class, and major.
- Don't read off of your resume.
- Connect your experiences to explain how you ended up applying to this position.
- You don't need specific stories for this question.

2. Why Finance?
- Come up with at least two good reasons.
- Use examples or anecdotes to back up each reason.

3. Why the role?
- Come up with at least two good reasons.
- Use examples or anecdotes to back up each reason.

4. Why the firm?
- Come up with at least three good reasons.
- First reason should be the people. Name drop the people you networked with naturally.
- Second reason can be easily derived from the "letter to shareholders" from the CEO of the firm. The firm's values are usually written in these reports, so you'll be able to find an appealing point about the company.
- Third reason should be about why you're a good fit for the firm.

5. Technical: What's going on in the markets?
- Have a list of nine things going on the markets.
- Be able to explain any of these topics.
- If you're recruiting for sales and trading, be ready to present potential trade ideas that reflect your opinion on the topic.
- You don't need specific stories for this question.

6. Pitch a particular company you follow
- Select a company that is not well-known.
- Memorize the important numbers: P/E Ratio, stock price, etc.
- Understand the general trend of the asset, not just a snapshot.
- Keep the pitch short and concise with strong deliverables backed by evidence when needed.

7. What are your strengths and weaknesses?
- Come up with three qualities for each.
- Brainstorm the first three strengths that come to mind and ask around if you're having a hard time figuring them out.
- Don't come up with weaknesses that can be seen as a strengths like perfectionism or working too hard.
- Back up each strength and weakness with an example. You'll have six different stories for this question.
- Come up with real weaknesses, unless a weakness is directly detrimental to the role to which you're applying.
- Weaknesses don't have to be related to your habits or personality. A weakness can be something like poor coding skills or not speaking another language.

- For each weakness, make sure you explain how you're working to overcome it. Don't end your weakness without a solution.

8. Talk about a time you exhibited leadership
  - Come up with two different stories.
  - The best stories tend to be the first stories that come to mind.
  - You don't have to use both examples when asked but have different stories available that can be applied to other questions.

9. Talk about a time you've been challenged
  - Come up with two different stories.
  - The best stories tend to be the first stories that come to mind.
  - You don't have to use both examples when asked but have different stories available that can be applied to other questions.

10. Talk about an experience that sets you up to succeed in [role]
  - Brainstorm the three most important skillsets for the role.
  - Use these qualities to describe yourself as long as they're arguable.
  - You don't have to use all three examples when asked but have different stories available that can be applied to other questions.

11. Other behavioral questions
  - Always answer the question directly first and explain with an example that you haven't yet used during the interview.

12. Any questions for the interviewer?
- If you're a good questioner, you'll be able to come up with a clever question on the spot.
- If not, be prepared to ask questions personalized to the interviewer like, "What's the main function of your group?", "How did you know you wanted to come to this firm?", and "How have you liked your experience at the firm so far?"

TECHNICAL QUESTIONS

While behavioral questions are similar across industries and roles and can be prepared with a template, no template for technical questions exists, as they differ with each role. If you're applying to investment banking roles, you'll have to study what EBITDA, DCF, and LBO models are, whereas for sales and trading roles, you will be asked to answer quick math, probability, and/or market-related questions.

Interviewers ask technical questions to check if you have the basic technical knowledge required for the role. If you are applying to investment banking, you should know discounted cash flows, leveraged buyout models, and accounting measures, but if you are applying to sales and trading, you should know market trends, asset class behaviors, and even some probability. These questions are relatively easy to prepare, as online materials are available with a list of questions and concepts.

Another reason interviewers ask technical questions is to see how well you function under pressure. You'll most likely be asked some questions that test technical abilities over the minimum level required for the job, whether it be statistics, math, or finance. Interviewers want to see if you can maturely handle unexpected questions and startling situations. While it would be ideal to answer these questions correctly, interviewers don't expect them to be answered perfectly. The key is to stay calm and organized regardless of how clueless you are.

When asked a technical question, answer with full confidence and explain your logic and workflow. If you think the question falls under the first category of questions that test necessary basic knowledge but don't know the answer, apologize and let them know you can either follow up with them or explain what you might know that can be relevant to the question. If you're given a question that falls under the second category but don't know the answer, start off by asking them if you can have a few seconds to think the question through. This shows that you're controlled and mature. Within the given time, try to walk through your thought process on how you might potentially solve the problem. If you aren't able to answer the question, don't worry. You've already answered the question better than most candidates who reveal how vulnerable and anxious they become in an uncomfortable situation.

PRE-RECORDED VIDEO INTERVIEW

Video interview is usually the first interview. These can be as short as five minutes or as long as an hour. Companies now readily opt for pre-recorded interviews because of their low cost. Pre-recorded video interviews differ from in-person video interviews in that you're talking to the computer instead of a person. You'll be answering randomly generated questions from a question bank the firm has and won't be asked any follow-up questions. You'll also be given a limited number of chances to answer each question. Sometimes you're given one chance, but you may be given multiple chances. Other than these few technical differences, pre-recorded video interviews are similar to in-person interviews.

Most interviews will give you a set amount of time to think about your response. Have a notebook in front of you to jot down the ideas you're going to use from your idea bank. Once you choose your stories, use this time to think about how you're going to phrase them. Don't look at your notes while you're answering.

If you're given more than one chance to respond, optimize this opportunity. Re-recording your answers has no disadvantage. People aren't interested in how many attempts it took you to come to the final version of your response. If you are comfortable with your response after a few tries, continue to the next question.

GENERAL RULES FOR PRE-RECORDED VIDEO INTERVIEWS

- Treat this interview as if you were talking to a real person. One of the most common mistakes people make is thinking they can get away with reading pre-written answers on their laptops. People watching your video interviews can tell if you're reading off of something or if you have memorized your answers word for word. Both are undesirable.

- Pre-recorded video interviews are interviews. Find a private setting to record your interviews. I've heard some sad but funny stories of roommates and parents barging through the door in the middle of an interview. Lack of care and effort to find a private setting sends the message that you're careless, which is more than enough reason to drop you.
- Make sure you're properly dressed. The video will only reveal the top part of your body, so you can get away with non-professional attire in parts the camera doesn't capture. However, as I've said earlier, it's important to put yourself in the mindset of an in-person interview.
- Adjust the angle and the brightness of the camera and the height of your chair according to your setting so you're looking straight into the camera when you're talking. Also make sure to always look directly into the camera. A good way to think of this is to think of the lens of the camera as the eyes of your interviewer. Making eye contact is essential in any interview.
- Make sure to smile and look confident. This is the most important piece of advice for any interview. Even if you think you understand the importance of this, it's easy to get back to your natural posture and tone. People often start off with a bright smile but gradually lose their energy, smile, and confidence as they progress to the next question. Showing confidence and high energy can never go wrong and it really helps to build a positive impression.
- Lastly, make sure to confirm no technical issues will crop up: no missing laptop charger, malfunctioning camera, or muted microphone.

GENERAL RULES FOR IN-PERSON INTERVIEWS

- Go into the interview with positive energy and an attitude that conveys your excitement to have the chance to interview. It might be your only interview for the day, but interviewers across the table probably went through more than enough interviews evaluating similar people with similar answers. The most effective and easiest way to stand out is to have a good attitude during your conversations. It's hard to frown at a smiling face. Use this to your advantage.

- Print out several extra copies of your resume to show you're prepared. In rare cases, the resume they have is an outdated version or, for some reason, the resume was printed out incorrectly with a cut in the middle. Bring enough copies to hand out so you're prepared for the worst.

- Always remember that the person sitting behind the table interviewing you is also human. They have feelings just like you. Participating in the interview just as in any natural conversation is the best way to talk. If you treat the interview as an interrogation, you'll find yourself acting stiff and awkward.

- Be sure to ask for your interviewer's contact information, as these interviews are also a form of networking. Add them to your fiend list so you can follow up with them after the interview.

- Always be prepared to ask questions to the interviewer. As you can see at the end of the list of interview questions, I guarantee that the interviewer will ask if you have any questions for them. This is one of the hardest tasks during an interview but try to think of the interview as one of your usual coffee chats. The best way to answer this question is to ask a personalized question related to the interviewer. You can ask what they do at the firm, why they chose to stay at the firm, or anything else you genuinely find interesting to ask. Interviewers tend to like talking about themselves, especially after listening to other people talk for hours.

- Lastly, make sure to get good sleep the night before. Try to get to bed as early as possible so you get enough sleep for the day. Your condition matters tremendously, so don't underestimate the power of maintaining it.

- The rules for in-person interviews apply for phone interviews as well, which is why I don't have a separate section for phone interviews.

KEYS TO BECOMING A FIEND

- Understand the different types of interviews.
- Create an interview template to organize your stories for behavioral questions.
- Stay calm if you receive a technical question you don't know the answer to.
- Having a positive attitude is, by far, the most important tip in any interview.
- Practice, practice, practice.

CHAPTER 13

AFTER SUPERDAY

THE OFFER

I received a phone call from J.P. Morgan only three days after my Superday.

My heart began beating faster, yet I felt prepared—I steeled myself for the worst and hoped for the best. I picked up the phone from Mutt, who I knew was going to call to share the result. "Congratulations kid. You got it." The flurry of thoughts and emotions that accompanied the acceptance itself is a blur. Had I misheard him? No. I had gotten in. I barely kept myself in my seat. Tears and laughter somehow came simultaneously. I must have looked crazy as I repeatedly asked him if it was real. I signed immediately.

Today, the excitement of J.P. Morgan is dimmed, but walking in and out of the office reminds me of the work I had put in to get this job and makes me happy. Before I had read that coverless book, I had always imagined I would work in South Korea. I started off my recruiting journey as a blank slate. I knew nothing about finance, had no connections, and had only a vague desire to work on Wall Street.

NETWORKING AFTER THE OFFER

I joined J.P. Morgan as a credit training intern. Credit traders, to put it simply, work with corporate debt, which can be subdivided into Investment Grade, High-Yield, Distressed, and Credit Default Swaps. The summer was an intense learning experience. I was given the opportunity to learn all about the credit market, but I also learned that trading isn't a great fit for me. Thanks to my supportive team members, I was able to freely explore my interests and gain more exposure to different roles in the firm throughout the summer.

My networking game resumed. Over the ten weeks of summer, I sat with and had coffee chats with a little over 100 people from J.P. Morgan. I took my time to seriously consider my priorities and things I consider important in a job. I was then able to narrow down my options. After meeting with people on the team and shadowing the work done, I realized I would enjoy the work the Cross-Asset Structuring team does. I share this story to illustrate that your networking game doesn't end even after the offer. You never know how your preferences and priorities will change. Networking can and will help you with any transitions you go through.

IN WRITING THIS BOOK

Recruiting for Wall Street, and especially for J.P. Morgan, was a dream that initially seemed inconceivable. I've been through my ups and downs. I also had the chance to learn from my mistakes, which ultimately led me to write this book. I've included many tips, strategies, and suggested methods I've accumulated after talking with professionals on Wall Street.

I hope *The Undergraduate Fiend* serves as a cheat sheet for those who share the same dream I had. The true effect of this book will show when your ambitions and your enthusiastic mentality for your dream job combines with the technical advice in this book.

Many of the people I mentioned, such as Josh Jen, Hal Lin, Kevin Ma, Nick Hibshman, Man-Lin Hsiao, and Kevin Huang, all understood the importance of the concepts and tips written in this book.

I wrote *The Undergraduate Fiend* in hopes the book would guide those who need the help I once needed. I'm here to help and encourage your dreams. Feel free to reach out through email at *theundergraduatefiend@gmail.com* or through the blog *theundergraduatefiend.home.blog* if you have any questions. I promise to try my best in answering your questions and providing the help you need.

I sincerely hope for your dream to come true.

KEYS TO BECOMING A FIEND
- Enjoy the moment when you receive the offer.
- Networking never ends.
- Don't merely read the book as a guide. Put it into practice.
- Don't hesitate to reach out when you need help.

RECOMMENDED READINGS

———

1. Megan Gebhert's *52 Cups of Coffee*
A book that shares stories of fifty-two different coffee chats
with businesspeople and others over a year

2. Michael Lewis's *Liar's Poker*
A hilarious book that describes the day at Salomon Broth-
ers during the '70s and '80s

3. Burton Malkiels's *A Random Walk Down Wall Street*
A great source for understanding market fundamentals
and different types of investments

4. Benjamin Graham's *The Intelligent Investor*
A classic stock market bible on value investing shared by
Benjamin Graham, one of the greatest investment advisers
of the twentieth century

5. Andrew Ross Sorkin's *Too Big to Fail*

A gripping narrative of the drama behind the 2008 financial crisis revealing the details and specifics behind the scenes

6. Roger Lowenstein's *When Genius Failed*
An exciting narrative on the rise and fall of Long Term Capital Management

7. John Rolfe and Peter Troob's *Monkey Business*
A comedic description of the lives of two investment bankers that unveils the true lifestyle of working on Wall Street

8. Michael Lewis's *The Big Short*
An exciting story that shares the happenings while the economy crashed in 2008 and how a few smart people made a lot of money

9. Jack Schwager's *The New Market Wizards*
A book that shares live interviews with successful traders with different strategies and backgrounds who all have valuable lessons to share for those who dream to work in the markets

10. Lasse Pedersen's *Efficiently Inefficient*
A textbook written in non-textbook format that teaches readers all about financial market behavior and key trading strategies from hedge funds